The Salmon Bank

An Ethnohistoric Compilation
by
Jacilee Wray

Anthropologist
North Coast and Cascades Network
for
San Juan Island National Historical Park

March 1, 2003

"Persons supplied with the proper appliances for carrying on a fishery
might find it a profitable occupation"

"At night all the Purseine boats used to anchor in Griffin Bay and some of the men would come up to the house and sing. Uncle George played the violin and Aunt Annie the piano. Uncle Frank called for the square dances."

Caption on back of trap photo by Bill Jakle

Picnic below Boyce place 1938

A special thank you to Bill Jakle for sharing his incredible knowledge and photographs

Table of Contents

Introduction

Over the past three years, the following information has been collected and compiled by Jacilee Wray, anthropologist at Olympic National Park. Included here are excerpts from interviews with several long-time residents of San Juan Island who have specific knowledge about the Salmon Bank off of South Beach at San Juan Island National Historical Park. Archival research was also conducted at the Center for Pacific Northwest Studies in Bellingham, as well as collecting and reviewing published accounts, and locating and scanning historic photos. This information has been compiled so that park staff can understand the cultural importance of the Salmon Bank and identify further research.

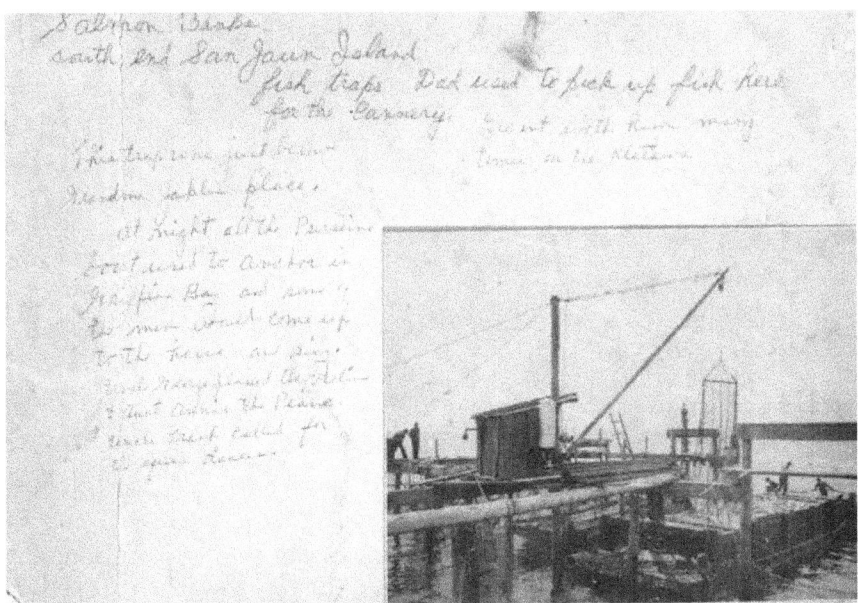

Summary of Salmon Bank History

San Juan Island emerged from the last glacial period around 13,000 years ago. The great moraines left behind by the glacial ice formed a submerged ridge, known as the Salmon Bank (Stein 1994:11-1). If people occupied the island soon after the glacial ice retreated, archeologists have yet to discover their remains. Perhaps because the ocean level has risen since that time, leaving archeological evidence submerged. Archeologists do know that people inhabited the island about 5,000 years ago, around the same time that important resources like the western red cedar and the Pacific salmon stabilized (Bergland 1988:38). Archeological evidence of habitation and harvesting of marine resources increases by 2,500 years ago. The people living at South Beach may have been weaving fiber for reef nets with the whale bone whorl found within the Maritime Phase (2500 to 1500 BP) of the Cattle Point site by Arden King in 1946 (King 1950; Stein 2000:49). Arden King states that the Salmon Bank "constituted a powerful factor in the regular occupation of the Cattle Point site" (King 1950:3).

In historic times we know the Indian reef net fishery was well established off the islands and in 1850, James Douglas, the manager of the Hudson Bay's installation at Fort Victoria, decided to explore the potential for trade with the Indian fisherman of San Juan Island. "William McDonald was sent to the southern tip of the island where the natives had set up extensive systems of reef nets on the shoals" (Bailey-Cummings 1987:21-22). A Hudson's Bay fishing camp was located at what is known today as Grandma's Cove, in either 1850 or 1851. Wayne Suttles (1998:38) conducted a study for the NPS on historic fishing locations, and concluded that the location of the HBC salmon fishery is uncertain, as there are reports that it could have been at Eagle Point or Fish Creek, as well as Grandma's Cove. It appears from Charles John Griffin's 1854 journal that the HBC moved its fishery station that winter. Griffin notes on April 8th that a band of Klallam are at "my old encampment" waiting for the salmon fishery. On July 12th Griffin reports that the station [perhaps the new fishing station] is at the small prairie at the end of Cowitchen Road[1]. This is a different location from the sheep encampment, which he identifies at the oak prairie. On September 3rd Griffin sets out to relocate to a winter station and finds "no place more convenient in every way & none so well adapted for a winter station as the small prairie before coming to the Bridge." On September 18th they "commence" to open the road from the shore of "Grande Bay" to the proposed winter station and on November 27th the "Men & Ind[s]" are all at the new station (Griffin 1854).

There were many Indian camps in the area, as Griffin sent a notice to all Indian encampments at the different fisheries on July 13, 1854. He mentions the Klallam commencing their fishing in two journal entries (6/3/54 & 6/6/54). There is also a reference to the Klallam living[2] on the island in April of 1858 that relates to a request for American protection from their marauding (Flaggaret 1859). Griffin traded salmon with the Cowichan (8/26/54), Songhees (10/5/54), and Saanich (11/13/54), but the only reference found in Griffin's journal to the Indians fishing specifically for the HBC fishery is on June 9, 1854 noting Cowitchen Jack fishing for the establishment. According to a book by Bailey-Cummings and Cummings (1987:21-2) the English paid the Indians one blanket (worth about $4) for every 60 fish caught for the HBC operation. At McDonald's fishery camp workers salted 2,000 to 3,000 barrels of salmon per season. Presumably, the salmon was supplied by the Indians who had reef nets around San Juan Island west of Pile Point, at Deadman Bay, Andrews Bay, and Mitchell Bay; and Open Bay on Henry Island (Bailey-Cummings 1987:22).

There is considerable documentation of Native groups who had settlements, mostly seasonal, on San Juan Island in historic times.

In an Elwha Klallam interview conducted for Olympic National Park, Rosalie Brandt said her parents lived on San Juan Island on the "state side," which might mean the American side. Rosalie's sister was born on the island on September 11, 1896. Her mother, Josephine Sampson was from Saanich and her father Andrew Thomas was Lummi. They lived at Victoria Harbor and would come across to camp and dig clams on the island, where they "met a lot of Indians" (Brandt 1991).

In the first U.S. land claim testimony, Duwamish, et al. vs. U.S., depositions were taken from San Juan Island Indian residents, describing Indian village locations that they remembered in their lifetime, as well as changes in fish trapping[3] (Appendix D). The following summary reflects their testimony and includes the claimant's name and age in 1927.

---

[1] "Probably the town site of Friday Harbor, as Boyd Pratt has deduced from descriptions and map contained in Hunter Miller, San Juan Archipelago, UW, 1943, Wyndam Press, Vermont, in collection of SAJH" (Correspondence Mike Vouri 4/7/03).
[2] George Gibbs reported for the Northwest Boundary Survey that the Clallams occupied "a part of San Juan"; while "the whole inside, or north eastern part of San Juan, formerly belonged to a tribe kindred to the Lummies (sic) and now extinct." Gibbs suggested that the valuable fisheries would make this an "admirable" reservation in the future if it was "desirable" to remove these "tribes from the main" (Gibbs 1858).
[3] In 1880 there were 382 Indians in San Juan County and a white population of 948 (Hayner 1929:83).

F.D. Sexton, age 74, remembered events from 1859. He lived at Kanaka Bay and knew of Indians living on the Larson place in quite a few cedar plank and bark houses. Mr. Sexton said there was a "burying ground over there at our place," where they buried their dead in canoes on a little island and that when the tide was out you could walk across to it. In 1927 there were still several graves that could be seen on the banks. Indian houses were also located along the beach and at a place where "they used to come over on the side-from the other side to live and fish" [South Beach] (US 1927:428).

Alice Lighheart, age 56, remembered villages at Kanaka Bay and Mitchell Bay.

Jim Walker, age 69, said there were Indian houses at Kanaka Bay, including one big house and several smaller houses and there was one Indian house at Argyle (US 1927:455-6).

Cecelia Knowlsen, age 95, remembered Captain George, who they called Queana and Chief Seattlak. He lived in a house down by the Hudson Bay Post. The house was made of mat and boards and was located on the bank, close to the beach (US 1927:456-9).

John Dougherty, age 74, had lived on the island since 1865 and discussed the Indians fishing in the early days, until the white people put up fish traps at the locations where the Indians fished. When asked how many traps there were at this locality, he said there were quite a few of them, "mostly on the west side of the island" (US 1927:443).

Mr. Dougherty mentioned Indian houses he remembered in his early years: one up on Mitchell Bay, two or three down at the south end of the island, and "every little place used to have shacks of their own," all around the island. "Right across here they had one, on this reservation, on the beach there. Up here at the north there was one, besides Mitchells Bay. They didn't live on Griffin's Bay, they lived on the beach [South Beach] then and also down at what they call the south end, that is, on Hobbs Place[4]" (US 1927:442-4).

Stephen Gross, age 50, a San Juan Indian who had been fishing for 30 years in 1927, told the interviewers that 20 years ago there were 25 fish traps, while only 15 in 1927. In the early days the fish packing companies took up the old Indian fishing locations and drove the Indians away (US 1927:449-50).

Jane Williams, age 66, remembered villages on the north end of Roche Harbor, at American Camp, and down at the light station "was a little village there." She remembers buildings still habitable at Mitchell Bay, and at the wireless station at Cattle Point she saw houses that had their extant corner posts and roofing [presumably not wireless station built for WWI].

Mrs. Williams spoke of changes in salmon fishing. She said that the white people built their traps at the old locations where the Indians used to take their fish, and that the Indians had to go somewhere else to "get their living" as the white people drove them off and took their place. "They had to go somewheres, you know" (US 1927:437).

---

[4]1860 map shows Hubbs near Cattle Point. Paul Hubbs was a customs official who had several wives over time, including several Indian girls (Bailey-Cummings 1987:63-64).

Caroline Ewing, age 78, remembered a "big reservation" at Hobbs Point, and one at "the fort," in early times. Also "one below Peter Larson, and one below our place. Jimmy Fleming's place [**Map**], and one at Roach (sic) Harbor and scattered all along the beach that way, villages all through" (US 1927:439). She was asked if there were many Indians when she was a girl, and she replied "Oh, I say there was," and that they had their permanent villages all around. She remembered Captain George, who was "chief" on one side of the island," somewhere on Bald Hill. She said, she couldn't count all the villages, but "this little village" had 30 or 40 houses, and a big fish-drying building. She was asked if the house belonged to the people that lived in them and she said that they belonged to the tribe. "One will go and another will walk right in" (US 1927:438-442).

Caroline also responded to questions about fishing. She said it used to be thick with fish and that she had seen the Indians dry their fish, "you know, and it would stand so high, just like you would cut cordwood and cord it up, it was so thick. They just took out what they wanted and just threw the others away, but of course there was no white folks around to get the fish." Back then it was "nothing but the Indians." Now the fish are pretty scarce. When asked why, she replied that "if it wasn't for the traps of the whites--they caught them all away." They have traps all over the island at different places (US 1927:440-441).

With the numerous Indian fisheries to supply the HBC operation, the fact that the fishery had "fallen off" by 1859 is surprising (Gibbs 1859). Dr. C.B.R. Kennerly notes the end of the fishery in his 1860 report:

> In the vicinity of the southern end of the island are perhaps the best fishing grounds on Puget Sound. Great quantities of halibut, codfish, and salmon are taken by the numerous tribes of Indians who at the proper season resort to this vicinity for the purpose of fishing. The Hudson's Bay Company were formerly in the habit of putting up at this place from two to three thousand barrels of salmon alone which were bought from the natives. Persons supplied with the proper appliances for carrying on a fishery might find it a profitable occupation (Kennerly 1860).

Indian reef-net fishermen and settler families fishing with net or pole were probably the main types of fisheries at the Salmon Bank until the late 1880s when non-Indians began to harvest salmon with fish traps. The first fish trap on Puget Sound is documented in about 1880 at Point Roberts, for which the owner used the Indian reef-nets as a model, as the "leads duplicated that of the Indians" (Cobb 1930:483, 486). The fish traps were able to capture sockeye, which previously had to be caught in sheltered areas along the shore with seine and gill net (Rathburn 1900:340). Around 1892, Deblin[5], who started the cannery at Friday Harbor, had a trap outside of Fisherman's Bay, Lopez Island (Troxell Mason 1991:165). The trap was lauded as the "most efficient means of catching sockeye salmon," however it had the adverse effect of limiting access and productivity of tribal reef-net locations (Radke 2002:12). The impact on the reef-net is reflected in that by 1909 only five Indian reef-nets were still in use (Cobb 1930:487).

_____

[5] Cobb says the name was A.E. Devlin, who came from the Columbia River (Cobb 1921:19).

Washington state law required traps to be physically removed from the water during a part of each year beginning in 1892 (Morisset, et. al 1978). This meant that at the end of every season engineers had to precisely survey the pilings before removal, to ensure they would be placed in their exact (licensed) location the next spring (Mason Troxell 1990). The depth, length, and spacing requirements were set by the state, as were restrictions on acquisition and abandonment of sites. The mesh had to be greater than three inches and the lead shorter than 2,500 feet. The end passageway requirement was at least 600 feet and the lateral passageway at least 2400 feet between nets [Ballinger's Annotated Codes and Statutes of Washington, Sec. 3349, 3351, 3353, (1897)]. In 1898 and 1899 many fish trap locations "changed hands" as the big companies began purchasing trap locations (Cobb 1930:483). Section 3349 of Washington Statute decreed that no one person or corporation could own more than three trap sites. To circumvent the law, companies like PAF formed fish trap corporations. This is the reason for the diversity of names for trap licenses on San Juan Island as seen in Appendix A.

The cannery at Friday Harbor began operations in 1894 (Cobb 1921:19;Radke 2002:16). In March of 1899 the Pacific American Fisheries (PAF) purchased the Island Packing Company at Friday Harbor and it was renamed Friday Harbor Packing Company. This cannery was an important operation for the PAF until their corporate end in 1965 (Radke 2002:23-4). The cannery workers may have consisted of many local people, but they also employees Chinese laborers, as correspondence from 1901 refers to the Chinese working at the cannery and a cannery diagram shows "China house" [Chinese quarters] (PAF 1901b). 1903 correspondence indicates that there were also Japanese workers at the cannery, but they "got rid of" them (PAF 1903b).

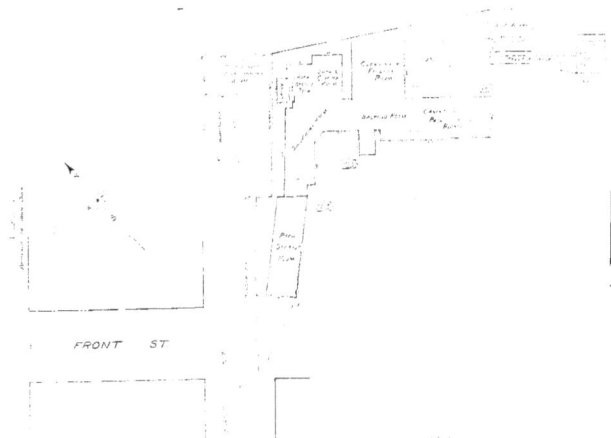

FRONT ST

In 1898 the PAF owned fifty fish traps and packed 70% of the Puget Sound[6] sockeyes (Radke 2002:24). By 1901 private owners had sold almost all of the fish trap locations to the big companies, some of the best locations selling for over $100,000. These locations became permanent fixtures of the cannery business, and were filed upon, surveyed, licensed, and worked on a specific schedule (Shield 1918:65). Sometimes dummy traps or non-working traps were set up to retain a licensed location. Crews would stage a catch at these dummy traps to comply with the law that required they be used within a seven year time period (Thorstenson 1995).

The sockeye salmon industry was bountiful, its biggest years were 1905 and 1909 (Radke 2002:95), but the best the PAF ever packed was 450,000 cases in 1913 (Radke 2002:160). PAF records at the Center for Pacific Northwest Studies provide catch records and some insight into the operation of the PAF Salmon Bank camp, operated by Friday Harbor Packing Co. and located below the spring at South Beach (See Map). James Burke was the superintendent of both the cannery and the trap camp at South Beach in 1900. On July 9, 1900 the cannery received 2,000 fish, resulting in 178 cases of sockeye, 35 cases of red spring and 8 cases of white spring (PAF 1900)

The following list comprises the grades of canned salmon with brands owned or controlled by Deming and Gould Co. or Pacific American Fisheries (Mitchell 1920:30-31).

Brands of Puget Sound Sockeye:	Brands of Puget Sound Chinook:	Brands of Puget Sound Cohoes:	Brands of Pinks	Brands of Chum

---

[6] Puget Sound is defined in the statute as "that portion of the tide waters emptying into the Straits of Juan de Fuca, and the bays, inlets, streams, and estuaries thereof." [Sec 7381 (1897)].

Blue Jay *Bow Knot* *Empress* *Glenwood* *Hindoo* *Jungle* *Kenmore* *Key City* *Oakleaf* *Pride of Ocean* *Red Poppy* *Red Rover* *Red Top* *Sport* *Uwanta* *War Eagle* *Warrior*	*Great Northern* *Royal Fisher*	*Autumn* *Chic* *Circle S* *Cycle* *D.A.R* *Easter* *Modoc* *Rock* *Southland* *White Rock*	*Clove* *Corsair* *Jap* *King Bird* *Minnehaha* *7-11* *Shell* *Stork* *Terrapin*	*Auk* *Harbor Light* *Humpty Dumpty* *Nautical* *Nile* *Raceland*
Sockeye [Red, Blueback, or Quinault] The most plentiful of all the species of salmon. Packed in July and August.	Chinook [Spring, King, Tyee, Quinnat] Packed in spring and summer.	Cohoe [Medium Red, Silversides] Packed in October	Humpback or Pink Salmon Packed in August and September	Chum [Calico, Keta, or Dog Salmon] Packed in November

There was often a discrepancy between the count of salmon at the trap site and the count at the cannery. On July 24, 1900 John Berg, camp manager, counted 7200 sockeye and 700 spring salmon at the trap, whereas the cannery counted 5790 sockeye and 540 spring. Superintendent Burke believed the cannery count the correct one because they were counted "into the tub" (PAF 1900a,b).

The camp at South Beach obtained their water from at least three locations between 1900 and 1903. In 1900 the PAF commissioned the steamer *Councilman* to tow a filled water scow to the Salmon Bank and the steamer *Michigan* brought the empty scow back (PAF 1900). William Jakle, Sr., operated the *Michigan* around 1900. In 1901 [Edward] Warbass presented PAF with "a bill for water" (PAF 1901a) and in 1902 payment of rental for the water right at the spring at Salmon Bank camp was made to Eliza Jakle for $50.00 (PAF 1902). In 1903 the Bellingham cannery requested that the San Juan Island manager "buy us a ton of old potatoes in good condition for use over here? Potatoes are very short on the Bay. New potatoes are worth about 2 cents per pound…. If you can secure a ton for us, please ship them as soon as possible, and try and arrange to have the steamer land at our Commissary dock (PAF 1903a).

South Beach, Courtesy Whatcom County Museum (WCM 7298)

South Beach views, Courtesy of Bill Jakle

Frank McLain was the cook at the camp in 1899. Receipts show that milk was being furnished to the pile and steamer drivers by Mrs. George Heidenreich, Bill Jakle's maternal grandmother. Mrs. Heidenreich indicated she could provide butter to the camp as well (PAF 1902a). The PAF paid rent to Warbass to draw the scows and pile driver below his house in the wintertime (PAF 1901a). Payment for driving the piles was made to the San Juan Trading Co. in 1901 and to John W. King for hauling the piles out in 1903 (PAF 1901; 1903).

In 1913 construction crews were building a railroad above the Fraser River in British Columbia and blasting operations created a rock slide at Hells Gate that cut off the sockeye salmon from their spawning grounds. Although some of the blockage was removed by the spawning season of 1914, the damage diminished the Puget Sound sockeye fishery, probably as a result of turbulent water (Cobb 1930:506). The last big year for trap fishing was 1917; this can be seen in the chart in Appendix B. (Radke 2002:90).

Big companies, especially Alaska Packers Association, and Pacific American Fisheries had monopolized the salmon fishing industry. The cost of the trap installation every year and the exclusive rights of canning the salmon dissuaded independents. But even for the large companies, the profit margin was decreasing. Between the smaller return of Fraser River sockeye and competition with an ever-increasing fleet of new and improved purse seiners, traps became secondary in importance. In 1918 a trap operation cost, on average, $12,000 (Shield 1918:65). In 1924 the PAF declared, "forget the sockeye. If we can forget the sockeye, I think there is a chance of building up the salmon industry with the cheaper fish..." (Radke 2002:116).

Regulation

In order to save the fishing industry, several state initiatives were proposed to restrict certain types of fishing operations. In 1924, initiative 51 would restrict the taking of fish to hook and line or troll or gill net. Four years later Initiative 55 would abolish both purse seines and fish traps. These two initiatives failed and the trap fishery didn't anticipate the passage of any future initiatives.

As the purse seine became more competitive with the fish trap animosity grew between the two groups. The purse seiners felt that they were victims of a colonial empire as the fish trap industry owned everything from trap to can, and seemed to care little for conservation (Thorstenson 1995; Radke 2002:143). In 1934 purse seiners and sports fisherman aligned against the trap fishery with anti-fish trap initiative No. 77 to bar fixed appliances (Radke 2002:143). Widespread resentment of fish traps led to the passage of the initiative with 65% of the votes (Radke 2002:118,144).

It was difficult for cannery packers to make a living after the fish companies lost "their medieval control over fish and labor costs" (Radke 2002:163). The San Juan Island fishing community felt the loss of the traps as jobs dependent on the trapping industry, from pile driver to brailer, were gone. One of the two canneries in Friday Harbor began canning peas around 1925. Family farms became even more crucial, and fishermen who could afford their own boat became purse seiners or gill-netters. The prominent view was that the trap was not the problem, it was the monopoly[7]. With the rising operational costs for canning, and the capacity to fresh freeze salmon, the canned salmon was no longer a household staple. When the fish trap was outlawed in 1934, a trap's value went from $300,000 to one hundred dollars (Radke 2002:118,144).

The story of the Salmon Bank does not stop here. The increase in purse seining after traps were outlawed, the Boldt decision, the proliferation of farmed salmon, and the quiet loss of commercial salmon fishing because of threatened and endangered stock (Martin 1994:107) are all topics to be considered for further research. In this compilation of text and research materials the park will find information to better understand the Salmon Bank's trap fishing history, and its place in the park's cultural milieu.

---

[7] The fish trap has been considered as an alternative to gillnet fishing on the Columbia River as a means to harvest only those stalks of salmon that are not threatened and endangered (Martin 1994:126).

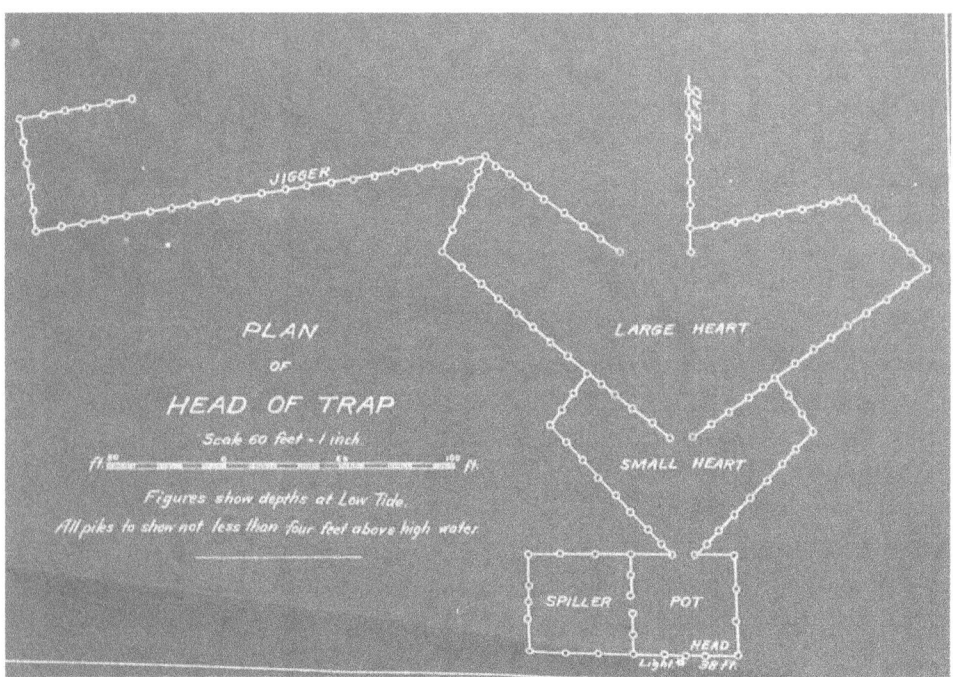

PLAN
OF
HEAD OF TRAP
Scale 60 feet - 1 inch.
Figures show depths at Low Tide.
All piles to show not less than four feet above high water.

JIGGER LEAD LARGE HEART SMALL HEART SPILLER POT HEAD

How a Trap Works

"The principle of entrapment was involved in the operation of the fish trap or pound net. The fish trap was an arrangement of piling, netting, and timbers. These were all attached in a manner that trapped the salmon. The trap was stationary, based on the piling being pounded into the sea bottom….

The fish trap was constructed employing knowledge of the habits of salmon. A migrating salmon will always forge ahead. Even when trying to get around obstacles, the salmon will never turn back in its wake. Thus, the fish trap was constructed across the path of a fish run. The lead was a combination of piling with timbers, and from the timbers netting of tarred wire hung forming the obstacle to the salmon's progress upstream. This obstacle began at the shore side and led the salmon to the heart of the trap, either one or a series of inverted "V's" forcing the salmon into the pot. The pot or pound as it was known in Europe, was a rectangular shaped corral constructed also of piling, timber, and netting. The salmon were led from the pot to the spiller from which they were dipped, or brailled, out into a scow or tender and carried off to the cannery. The fish trap was a maze-like construction leading the fish to capture."

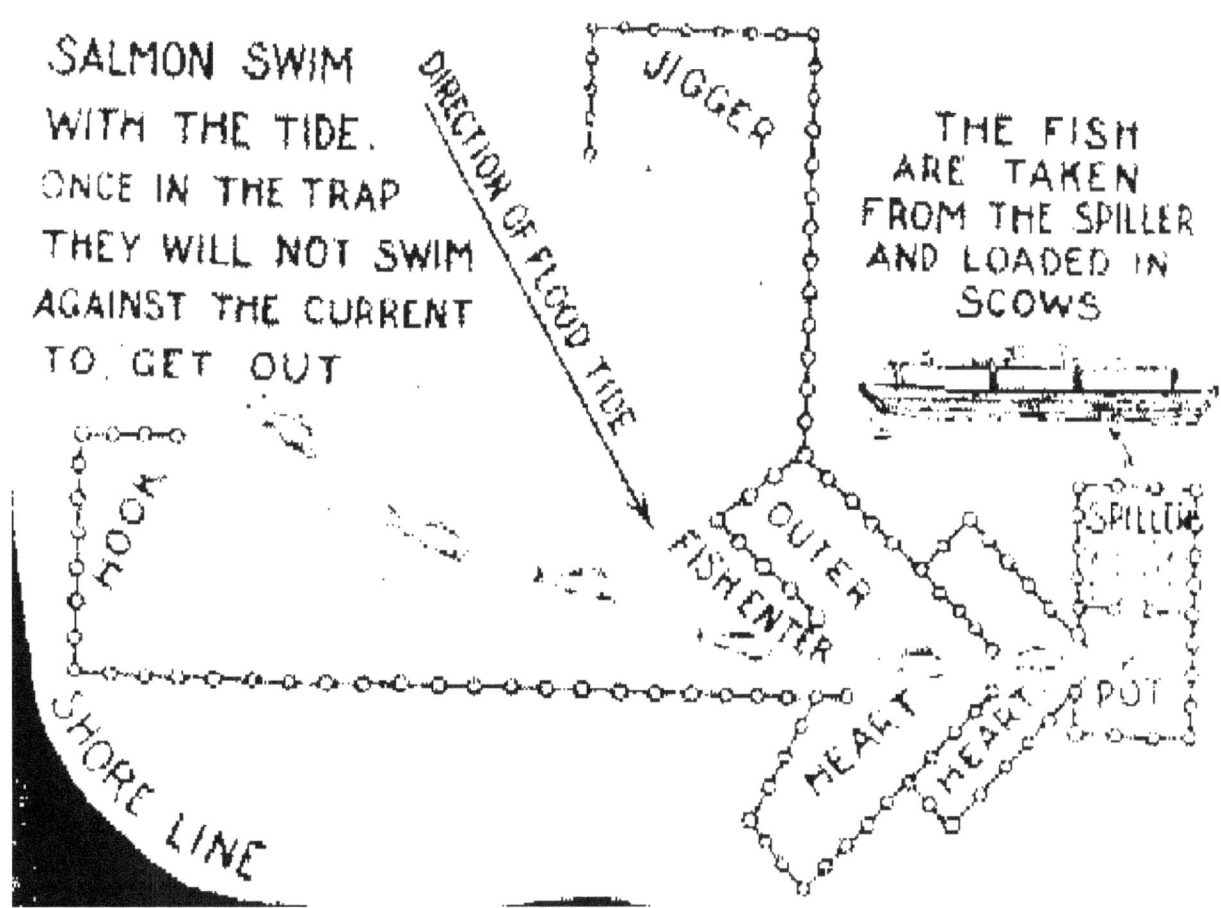

"The fish trap was the most efficient means of catching a large commercial supply of salmon. This enabled the cannery to maintain a cheap and stable supply of the resource. The construction of fish traps was a complex operation, entailing the use of men, materials and machinery" (Radke 2002:9-10).

"A trap is a stationary device. In its construction piles and stringers and wire or web netting are used. The lead consists of a single row of piles starting from and about at right angles to the shore. These piles are driven about ten to fifteen feet apart and wire netting is hung on them from above high water mark to the bottom. This netting is held down by means of weights. The lead reaches out to a little beyond the hearts, which are formed of two opposite rows of piling, running angularly presenting the appearance of two "V's," one beyond the other. Like the lead, these hearts are furnished with wire netting. The larger heart, that is the one nearer the shore, is named the "outer heart" and the smaller one is the "heart." The construction of these heart contrivances is such that the schools of fish which have followed the lead are directed into the tunnel formed at the junction of the heart and the pot. This tunnel terminates in a long, narrow opening running up and down. The apron is a sheet of web stretched from the bottom of the heart up to the pot in order to lead the fish when swimming low in the water into the tunnel.

The pot is a square compartment, 44x44 feet, formed of piling and containing a large dip net fastened on all sides to the pilling. It is about 2500 feet from the shore in water about 65 feet deep at low tide.

Alongside the pit is a similarly constructed compartment known as the "spiller." A small tunnel leads from the pot to the spiller. The fishing is done from the spiller at which time said small tunnel is closed.

At fishing time a large deck scow is lined up alongside of the spiller and beyond it a trap steamer furnished with a brailer operated by steam. Within the spiller is a stationary scow upon which fisherman stand, seven or eight in number, and raise by hauling the large dip net, about forty feet square. The brailer, which is a dip net on a smaller scale, being 12x12 feet in size, dipping over into the net thus raised, takes up hundreds of fish at a time and by means of steam-operated tackle dumps them on the deck of the scow. [Scows are owned by the cannery]

Brailing goes on until the spiller is emptied of thousands of fish, possibly. The large scow is capable of holding 12,000 Sockeyes. It is towed by the trap steamer to the next trap where like proceedings are had, as above" (Shield 1918:24).

"Some traps have jiggers and hooks, which are extensions of the outer heart and the shore end of the lead, receptively. These are first aids in turning the fish in the desired direction. Traps are built on the theory that the fish have a tendency to follow the shore line or an artificial construction and never turn back in their course. When they strike the lead they stay by it until they enter the labyrinth commencing with the outer heart. Here their fate is sealed and what becomes of them afterward we shall proceed to consider" (Mitchell 1920:13-14).

At the cannery as they are going up the elevator conveyor "a man stands near by with a little adding machine by means of which he records, by species, the number of salmon delivered'" (Mitchell 1920:15).

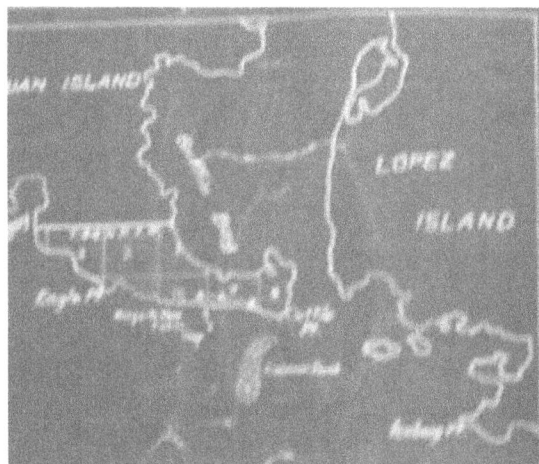

THE SALMON BANK

References

Bailey-Cummings, Jo and Al Cummings
1987 *San Juan: The Powder-Keg Island*. Beach Combers, Inc. Friday Harbor, Washington

Bergland, Eric and Jerry Marr
1998 Prehistoric Life on the Olympic Peninsula: The First Inhabitants of a Great American Wilderness. Pacific Northwest National Parks and Forests Association

Brandt, Rosalie
1991 Interview by Jacilee Wray for Olympic National Park. May 23, 1991

Cobb, John N.
1921 Pacific Salmon Fisheries. U.S. Bureau of Fisheries Document 902, Department of Commerce. Washington D.C.: United States Government Printing Office

1930 Pacific Salmon Fisheries. U.S. Bureau of Fisheries Document 1092, Department of Commerce. Washington D.C.: United States Government Printing Office

Duwamish, et. al vs. Washington
1927 Court of Claims of the United States. No. F-275. The Duwamish, Lummi, Whidby Island Skagit, Upper Skagit, Swinomish, Kikiallus, Snohomish, Snoqualamie, Stillaguamish, Suquamish, Samish, Puyallup, Squaxin, Skokomish, Upper Chehalis, Muckleshoot, Nooksack, Chinook, and San Juan Islands Tribes of Indians, Claimants, vs. The United States of America, Defendant

Flaggaret, J.M.
1859 Letter to General Harvey: Commissioner in Chief of the Pacific Division of the United States Army. From J.M. Flaggeret and Samuel McCauley. Dated July 11, 1859. National Archives

Griffin, Charles John
1854 Hudson Bay Company Post Journals Belle Vue Sheep Farm (transcribed by Mike Vouri, SAJH)

Gibbs, George
1858 Letter to Lieut. Jno. G. Parke (Chief Astronomer, &c, NW Boundary Survey). February 25, 1858. National Archives, DC RG46, Northwest Boundary Survey, Box 20, File E223

1859 Report of George Gibbs, Geologist, of an Examination of San Juan Island and of the Cowitchin Archipelago and Channel. Addressed to Archibald Campbell, Esq., U.S. Comm. N.W. Boundary Survey, March 18, 1859

Hayner, Norman S.
1929 Ecological Succession in the San Juan Islands. Publications of the American Sociological Society, 23:81-92

Kennerly, Dr. C.B.R.

  1860 Report of Dr. C.B.R. Kennerly of Reconnaissance of the Haro Archipelago, February 20, 1860. Geographical Memoir of the Islands between the Continent and Vancouver's Island in the vicinity of the Forty Ninth Parallel of North Latitude

King, Arden

  1950 "Cattle Point: A Stratified Site in the Southern Northwest Coast Region" in *Memoirs of the Society Form American Archaeology* No. 7. The Society of American Archaeology and the Tulane University of Louisiana. Menasha, Wisconsin.

Martin, Irene

  1994 *Legacy and Testament: The Story of Columbia River Gillnetters*. Washington State University Press, Pullman

Mitchell, C.M.

  1920 *From Trap to Can*. Secretary Pacific American Fisheries and Deming and Gould Co. Revised Edition

Morisset, Schlosser, Homer, Jozwiak, and McGaw

  1978 *Washington's Resistance to Treaty Indian Commercial Fishing: The Need for Judicial Appointment*. October 1978. http://www.msaj.com/papers/commfish.htm

PAF Correspondence, Washington State Archives, Northwest Region

  1900   To PAF from James Burke, Supt., July 11, 1900

  1900a To Thomas Hudson, Fairhaven, from James Burke, Supt., July 27, 1900

  1900b To Thomas Hudson, Fairhaven from James Burke, Supt., September 19, 1900

  1901   To Thomas Hudson from James Burke, Supt., June 5, 1901

  1901a To Thomas Hudson from James Burke, Supt., November 22, 1901

  1901b To Thomas Hudson from James Burke, Supt. June 5, 1901

  1902   To James Burke from Thomas Hudson, January 16, 1902

  1902a To Thomas Hudson, auditor from E. H. Nash, May 20, 1902

  1903   To B.W. Huntoon, Supt. from E.H. Nash, October 26, 1903

  1903a To E.H. Nash from Huntoon, July 7, 1903

  1903b To E.H. Nash, from unknown signature, PAF Fairhaven, August 25, 1903

  1918   The Shield: Official Publication of the Employees of Pacific American Fisheries and Allied Companies. Col. 1, No. 8. Annual Edition, December 1918. Center for Pacific Northwest Studies, Box 114

Radke, August C.

2002 *Pacific American Fisheries, Inc.: History of a Washington State Salmon Packing Company, 1890-1966*. McFarland and Company, Inc. Jefferson, North Carolina

Rathburn, Richard

  1900 A Review of thee Fisheries in the Contiguous Waters of the State of Washington and British Columbia. Report of Commissioner of Fish and Fisheries. Western Americana

Stein, Julie
1994 "Geoarchaeology of Sites on San Juan Island, Washington" Geologic Fieldtrips in the Pacific Northwest. Geological Society for America Annual Meeting Swanson, D.A. and R.A. Haugerud editors

2000 *Exploring Coast Salish Prehistory: The Archaeology of San Juan Island.* University of Washington Press, Seattle

Suttles, Wayne
1998 Prehistoric and Early Historic Fisheries in the San Juan Archipelago Prepared for the National Park Service, May 1998

Thorstenson, Bob
1995 *The Days of Salmon Traps and Fish Pirates: Tall Tales from the Fishing Grounds of Yesteryear.* Produced in conjunction with Semiahmoo Park Museum, Whatcom Parks and Recreation Foundation. John Sabella and Associates, Incorporated

Troxell Mason, Beryl
1991 *John Franklin Troxell, Fish Trap Man Puget Sound and San Juan Islands, Washington 1894-1934*

Bill Jakle Interviews
"San Juan Island was a fishing community"

The following are excerpts from five interviews with Bill Jakle: September 30, 2001, January 5, 2002, February 19, 2002, August 31, 2002, and February 16, 2003. I have consolidated the information by subject matter. Some of the sentences have been edited to complete them or to take out repeated words. Bill Jakle provided all photographs, unless otherwise noted. I have inserted portions of the Coast and Geodetic map downloaded from the UW web site to orient the reader. Information provided by Mike Vouri appears in brackets.

An Introduction to Bill Jakle's family

Both Bill's mother and father are from the area of American Camp. Sophie Cressie Amelia Hiedenreich was Bill's mother. She lived at the former Katz place at Old Town. Grandma and Grandpa--George and Marguerite Hiedenreich came from Oklahoma, via Tacoma and rented property from Katz and farmed. The English had pulled out by that time.

PHOTO OF VIEW OF KATZ FARM

PHOTO OF KATZ HOUSE

Bill's father, William was the son of John George Jakle and Eliza Furlong, who lived on the hill on the north side of Mt. Finlayson. Eliza was initially married to James Bryant. After he drowned in the lagoon, she remarried George Jakle. George and Eliza had five children together--George, William, Edward, Katie, and Eliza. Frank Bryant was the only child from Eliza's marriage to James Bryant.

PHOTO OF ELIZA'S HOUSE [Blow-up]

The original log house that Bill's dad was born in was moved up from the lagoon. It was a log cabin that Eliza and her first husband, James Bryant moved the cabin up the hill and built on to one end. This was the house where Eliza died. Bill's dad told him they got the cabin up the hill with a team of oxen. Bill can remember when he was just a boy, the old oxen yoke that hung between two trees on the north side of the gully, toward Mt. Finlayson. Two daughters of Eliza's died in their youth and were buried near the house. Two other daughters lived and married; they are Annie Berg and Eliza Lambert.

Bill's grandmother, Marguerite (Beck) Hiedenreich had two sisters, Katie and Minnie. Minnie was married to a man with the last name of Frank, and they lived across the road from the redoubt.

The following is from the interview:

JW: So let me get this straight where everybody lives. So down at Katz's place was your mom?

BJ: They farmed it, yes. They farmed it.

JW: What did they farm?

BJ: Well, I've got some of those pictures that I would like you to find. I can't find them. It shows my Grandpa and his two older sons shocking grain. Right there on that land right by the redoubt or whatever you want to call it. I could almost throw a rock from the redoubt into [Minnie's] yard. Well I know that I could throw it into her yard.

PHOTO OF HAY STACKS [Heidenreich Farm]

PHOTO OF THRESHING GRASS [George Heidenreich at Katz Place]

PHOTO OF HAY WAGON KATZ PLACE

JW: On the side that's facing the...

BJ: The north side. There was quite a family. There were five daughters and one son of the Becks.

William Jakle and Sophie Hiedenrich had five daughters and one son, Bill. Marguerite married Brian LaBar. Edna married Fred Droullard. Marcella married Ernie Dougherty. Ruth married Vic Capron. Audrey is the youngest and she is still alive and living in Nevada. She was married to John Burton.

Bill's grandmother Eliza wsa married to James Bryant and had a son with him, Frank. James drowned in the lagoon, and Eliza lost the baby she was carrying while running to Old Town for help. Frank was given forty acres at South Beach, which he kept until he died. He was around 80 when he died, and he was born around 1860 - so this should be around 1940. Bill thinks he died before 1940.

JW: What happened to Bryant's property?

BJ: Well he had a... I'll get into a story here. Alfred Douglas, after my grandma and grandpa moved away from the Katz' place... Alfred Douglas, he was a farmer out on the island. He had a farm out right at the head of the valley and it's still known as the Alfred Douglas place out there. Douglas leased that property, the Katz' place. And he tried farming it and didn't make a go of it. That land grew lots of grass but unless you got rain at the right time it wouldn't grow crops. And he gave up and just used it for a sheep range when he had it. But he had a woman... I don't know where she came from, but he had a woman and he got her pregnant and she had a baby and he wouldn't marry her. And young Frank Bryant, he asked his mother to take her in and she wouldn't. I guess Frank must have been around marriageable age because he married her and made an honest woman out of her. And then he raised kids and his kids all worked in the fish camps when they got old enough. See they lived right there above the beach.

JW: Do you remember her name?

BJ Her first name was May. I don't know what her original name was.

JW: And what were their kids named?

BJ: The oldest boy was Clarence and Pete and Jim. That was the three boys that I remember. And then Nellie, the one that was Alfred Douglas's child. And he wouldn't claim her or marry her mother so she went by the name of Bryant. But she had all together about five or six kids. So Frank married May. Nellie died a single woman.

But Nellie was actually Alfred Douglas's... He couldn't deny her. He looked so much like her when she grew up. So he left his trademark.

Frank's kids lived there until they grew up and I don't know where they all went.

JW: Did you work there when any of them were there?

BJ: Well I didn't work there, I lived there. Dad used to grow potatoes on their [Frank Bryant's] property because it was real sandy soil and it grew wonderful potatoes. You could stack potatoes in your arm like stove wood almost. Big, long potatoes.

PHOTO OF GARDEN

JW: But you worked down there? Didn't you fish or do something down there?

BJ: Well I never worked there in the fishing industry. I was a kid and I used to go out on the traps with the people. Like I say, a lot of the young fellows that I knew that were going with my sister, or some of my sisters, something like that… It was a small island in those days. We knew everybody. And if I was going to the beach and they were going out on a trap I would get in the dory with them and go out with them. And pretty soon we'd come back. I've even eaten in the cookhouses a good many times. And the lifting crew, they lived right there. The fish companies had places for them that they lived.

JW: So the fish company must have rented or leased that land from Bryant didn't they?

PHOTO OF UNKNOWN MAN AROUND 1900 AT SALMON BANK SHACK

BJ: No.

JW: They didn't.

BJ: No because this was up the beach farther. It wasn't on Bryant's property.

JW: Oh it wasn't?

BJ: No it wasn't on his property. It was up toward Grandma's place. South, or east rather.

JW: Okay. Where the fish company had their camp.

BJ: Yeah. You see there were a good many fish companies.

JW: Who got the Jakle property?

BJ: George Jakle.

JW: George inherited it?

BJ: He didn't inherit it, he stole it. He was a drunkard, or alcoholic. And he got a bunch of his drinking friends and they made their Xs on it and said that they witnessed the will of the grandmother. That's how he got it.

JW: So after she passed away?

BJ: Yes.

JW: He altered the will?

BJ: He didn't alter it he just…

JW: He made one up?

BJ: Yes he just made up a will.

JW: Otherwise it would have gone to all the kids.

BJ: It would have gone to all of the kids.

JW: So then how long did he hang onto it?

BJ: Oh he hung onto it until he got it taken away from him.

JW: Oh he did?

BJ: Well he drank until he owed everybody on the island. Frank Bryant, her first son, he got forty acres that attached right below his mother's place. My Dad's brother George never worked. He stayed home with his mother and drank whiskey and partied. That was his reputation as long as I knew him or knew of him. And he died that way.

PHOTOS

Eliza

ADD Map of Jakle place and lagoon with grave

Eliza's wool

William Jakle, Bill's father

Two girls with dolls [Check with Bill to see if this is Annie and Eliza Jr.]

Group Portrait

Bills sisters and their husbands [Marguerite and Brian LaBar,
Edna and Fred Droullard, Ruth and Vic Capron, Marcella]

History of the Salmon Bank from Bill Jakle interviews

[The Hudson Bay Company established a Salmon Salting station at American
Camp in 1851. No permanent White settlers came to the island until after
1853 when Belle Vue farm was established. Eliza "Jeckle" (Jakle) is listed
as a native of Ireland in the 1870 census. Neither she nor her first
husband, Bryant are listed in the 1860 census. George and Eliza are listed
in 1870 census as farmer and wife with child, Frank Bryant, 6 years old]
(From Mike Vouri)

BJ: My grandmother was the original. She came over in about 1848. Eliza Furlong. Her first husband [James
Bryant] and her were going to homestead. They bought original acreage from -- [Charles Griffin?] The guy that
was head of the Hudson Bay Company over there and was in this sheep range. He sold them his place and then
they were going to homestead it. They didn't settle where the Hudson Bay was, they settled farther down on the
timbered side of Cattle Point.

Then the deal came up over who was going to get it, whether England was going to get it or whether United States and it dawdled so long that everybody surveyed it and laid it out in plots and everything, so they never got to homestead it. It got refused as far as homesteading.

[The federal government took a large portion of their property in 1876 to create a Coast Artillery Reserve](Mike Vouri)

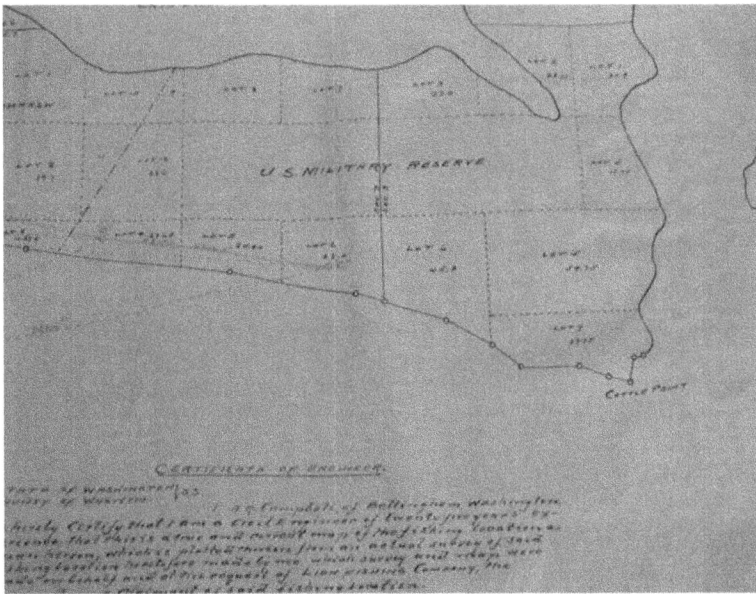

MAP SHOWS MILITARY RESERVATION

JW: They were going to homestead more than what they already purchased?

BJ: That's right. They had all of Cattle Point. They had around a thousand acres. That whole thing. You know where that little Old Town was, well, they went right over the hill to the Salmon Banks. They had that whole Cattle Point. Down toward the lagoon. That's where they settled. But when that guy [Griffin?] that built the house… He had that built and he lived in that. When the guy that was taking care of the Hudson Bay - they moved out and went up to the other end of the island - he sold out to my grandmother and Bryant. He sold that property, his house and what he had staked off and where the boundary line went across. It went from beach to beach practically, except on the little strip from Old Town, from the water up to where they had the line fence.

JW: Okay. So they owned the place where everybody fished at Salmon Bank? Your grandmother owned the Salmon Bank?

BJ: Well she didn't own the Salmon Banks; she owned a big part of the beach along up there. Her husband drowned and then she didn't marry my grandfather John George Jakle until around 1869.

JW: So what was John Jakle, what did he do in the war there?

BJ: He just was in the Army, that's all. It must have been quite a while after Bryant's drowning that she married my grandfather. I never did know whether that Bryant was with Pickett or not. [No, he came later with another company] (Mike Vouri)

My grandfather, John George Jakle was listed in the army as Yakely as I understand it and then the guy that was doing the book keeping changed it to Jakle. That's the way the story has been told. (A photo Bill has shows it spelled Yeackly)

[He was listed as Iakle, 21 years old, married and from Wurtemburg, Germany. In the same census he is listed as George Jakle, 29, married to Eliza. He from Wurtemburg, she from Ireland.](Mike Vouri)

27

JW: So she met him, because he was there at that camp?

BJ: Well, she owned that land. She bought the original from… If I could get back into the papers I could probably tell you more about… But this guy worked for the Hudson Bay Company and he was with the British. All that country there was sheep country. You know what I mean; it was open and grazing country. The HBC claimed it first and in the early days, the Indians showed some of the HBC how to catch fish on the Salmon Banks.

JW: Could you tell me about the early fishing on the Salmon Bank? What you know of the earliest fishing out there.

BJ: I can remember how it worked. In the winter time they would cut piling for all these traps and they knew what the depth of the water was and they cut piling so the shorter piling would go in first. As they got out into deeper water, why that would be the longest piling, except for the piling that they built the traps out of.

JW: Would they have to redo it every year?

BJ: Every year. They drove those piles in the spring and they hung the wire on them and they put the nets in and everything like that. Then in the fall they cut all that wire down and went to the bottom and then they would pull the piling out and keep them segregated. They start with the beach and take the shorter ones and they kept them all so when they drove them back again they would know which order they went in.

JW: So did your grandmother own that property? Salmon Bank, South Beach? Was that her land too?

BJ: She claimed everything to the water line.

JW: So did they have to pay her to access it?

BJ: No, I don't think they paid access. Because in those days whoever had the trap in there, he actually…. Heck, I can remember when I was a kid they had 60 men, at least, on those lifting places. And they had cookhouses and bunkhouses on South Beach.

JW: On her property?

BJ: No, just on the beach. Nobody claimed that[8].

JW: Like in the tidal area.

BJ: Yeah, above high water. They had big cookhouses there. They cooked probably for 60-70 people.

JW: Did the people live in tents you said?

BJ: Some of them. Some of them, they built shacks.

---

[8] In 1901 PAF Friday Harbor Superintendent James Burke writes Thomas Hudson, auditor in Fairhaven that the County Treasurer "states the tide lands in front of Lots 2-3-4 & 5 were not assessed to you and that he had same put on the books after receiving your list of property..." (PAF 1901). On July 3, Superintendent Burke received the deed for the tideland (PAF 1901a).

PHOTO OF TRAP MEN AND SHACK

JW: So what year is that.

BJ: In my lifetime. I can remember real well. I was born in 1915, so I can remember probably from 1921 or 22, from then on.

JW: And you said the Indians showed the first people about the salmon bank?

BJ: The English were there first. And they claimed that for their sheep ranch.

JW: But the HBC people fished too?

BJ: Well, not that I know of. Because that was settled long before I was born.

[HBC purchased and salted the fish and shipped to the Russian American Company until about 1859] (Mike Vouri)

1860 MAP SHOWS FISHING STATION NEAR JAKLE'S LAGOON

BJ: Frank Bryant, he was one of the early men in it.

JW: Bryant did this type of fishing?

BJ: Yes, he was on the fish traps. Dad [William Jakle] did too and George and Ed. They grew up right there. That's all that they knew was fishing. My dad was on the boats and things all his life.

(Children of Eliza and John George Jakle - George, William, Edward, Eliza, Annie [Mary A., married John Berg])

PHOTO OF BILL JAKLE SR. AROUND 1905

JW: Was it good money?

BJ: Not like it was in later years. At the time, they made wages.

JW: So would they work for one specific company?

BJ: Most of them, yes. If you worked for Alaska Packers, that's who you worked for. Or Friday Harbor Packing Company or PAF.

JW: Who did your dad work for?

BJ: He worked for Friday Harbor Packing Company most of the years that I remember. Then in later years, after he sold his boat, then he worked for anybody he could get a job with as skipper on a boat. I've got a picture of his boat out in the kitchen in about 1912 or 13. *Klatawa*.

PHOTO OF *KLATAWA*

JW: So he fished with that boat?

BJ: Well he was a cannery tender with it. He hauled fish with it, hauled the scows where they would load the fish. They would load it into the boat and they would load it into the scow too if there was more fish than what the boat could haul. They would keep track of what it was you know. They would call in to the cannery or somebody would let them know how heavy a bunch of fish was coming.

JW: So when did he have time to take the people on excursions to Sucia?

BJ: Well they didn't lift every day.

JW: Did they have specific days that they could fish?

BJ: Oh yeah.

JW: Back then even?

BJ: Yeah. They quit; I think, Friday afternoon at 4 o'clock if I remember correctly and I think that I do. And then they couldn't fish again until Sunday afternoon.

JW: They'd take weekends off?

BJ: Um hum.

JW: How long were the seasons. When did this operation start?

BJ: That would start in March to get the piling off the beach and it wouldn't end until September or later.

JW: How many different species of salmon?

BJ: Every specie that there was. They were after the sockeye fish, the choicest fish. The sockeye were the first fish that ran. And then salmon would run clear to the fall. The last fish was the dog salmon. They got the Humpies [pink] and the dog [chum] salmon, silver [coho] salmon, the king salmon and sockeye.

JW: The first fish traps, were they owned by a fishing company? Who were they owned by?

BJ: Oh gosh, Alaska Packers, San Juan Fish Company, Troxell, I could go on for half of a day to name them all, if I could remember all the names.

JW: And those went back all the way to Bryant's time?

BJ: Oh yeah. Not the original Bryant, no. To his son, Frank Bryant.

JW: So Frank was still around there.

BJ: That's all he ever did all his life was in the fishing. All the houses were out here along the beach. That's where all the lifting crews were. And the cookhouse and everything. It was all on this side.

JW: This is… I'm not sure where we are. It's hard to tell. I don't see this rock in this picture.

BJ: Well maybe we didn't get that rock in that picture.

JW: Okay so this is this rock right here? I think.

BJ: Could be. That very well could be.

JW: And then is this the Alaska Packers? This one?

BJ: Well I can't tell you exactly. This doesn't look like Grandma's house. This must be taken someplace else along here. There were so many traps along here. But this isn't Grandma's house.

JW: No, you don't see the big hill.

PHOTO OF SOUTH BEACH SHOWING TRAP CAMP AND DORIES, ELIZA'S HOUSE ON HILL

CLOSE-UP OF CAMP

SAME LOCATION IN 2003 by Jacilee Wray

BJ: You can see just about… I think that's Grandma's house right there, if I see good enough.

JW: When I get back I'm going to get a magnifying glass and look at that. So there sure are a lot less trees in this photo, and whose house did you say this was?

BJ: This is Frank Bryant's.

JW: Oh that's Bryant's.

BJ: That's got to be his house because you look right from Grandma's right down on it. He had forty acres down in there. Dad used to grow potatoes. Gee they made the most beautiful potatoes that you ever wanted to see.

When her son got old enough by her first husband, Frank Bryant, he got forty acres that attached right below his mother's place. He got forty acres there and whatever you do when you get land, and that's all he was allowed there, was forty acres. And that was right above the beach. See that was the only industry there, in those days, was the fishing industry. And he lived right above the beach, and they had all those fish traps along there. He was a beach foreman for I don't know which company. He may have worked for two or three different ones over the years. But in the early days they used to have a big cookhouse on the beach where they fed the men that were... They called them the lifting crews that lifted and got the fish out of the traps.

You know this here if you look real close - I should have a magnifying glass - but there are a lot of houses along here. So I don't know just exactly where that was taken.

JW: Is this fence... Was this her property line fence?

BJ: Grandma's, if it went, the fence would have come out way over here someplace. I don't know what the heck that is. It might be a fence. Somebody might have put a fence across here, I'm not saying that it isn't, but it isn't from Grandma's.

JW: And so Alaska Packers, what were you telling me about Alaska Packers?

BJ: Well they had their trap right close here.

JW: Right by here?

BJ: And it went straight out.

JW: From about where this rock is?

BJ: Yeah, just a little. So you know what I mean was that it wasn't right up against the rock.

JW: Just right in there?

BJ: It was probably fifty or sixty feet away from the rock where the pilings started. And then they went right straight out. Or I would say that as much as I can remember they were straight out. It might have been at an angle too.

MAP OF TRAP AT PACKER ROCK

PHOTO OF PACKER ROCK 2003 by Jacilee Wray

JW: So there was nothing right down in this little open area?
[Maps show Indian houses below Jakle's on the beach in this open area in 1897. Note the family portrait at the beginning of this document. The two women on the right appear to be Native American.]

BJ: Not that I ever remember. No houses or anything like that. Everything was on the beach here, the cookhouse and places. If you look at… Well we'll look again some time. You can see how many of those dories were pulled up on the beaches out of those two pictures.

JW: The ones that we were just looking at?

PHOTO OF SOUTH BEACH FROM ELIZA'S HOSUE AND 2003 PHOTO by Jacilee Wray

MAP SHOWS FISH BANK HUTS

BJ: Yeah. Here these are all just dories for the men that were working on traps. Do you remember those boats that we were looking at yesterday? I don't see any… Yeah, here's a boat here, way down here on that one there. There's a small boat.

JW: Oh yeah, I see it.

BJ: But all the traps, that's what they had. They always had two or three dories for each trap.

JW: So I think that we are right down here.

BJ: Well we could be. We could be. This is where the old Alaska Packers trap was anyway. And right on that side, on the other side, you asked me if there were any houses there, the San Juan Fish Company was the next trap on that side of the road. You can even see dories on the beach on the other side of the rocks there. And do you see all of the houses and things? Well those are the cookhouses and the bunkhouses for all of those crews that I told you. And that's all that they did was lift those traps.

MAP OF SAN JUAN FISHING CO. TRAP

JW: And is this Bryant's house here? Is that where his house would have been?

BJ: It would be over here someplace. This would be looking down from Grandma's house to the spring. And this is where the spring was, in this grove of trees right there. And you walked over the driftwood. I walked in there many times. And we were at the beach.

BJ: Frank Bryant's daughter, my dad's half brother, his family, the girls especially, worked in those cookhouses. [Mother May, children Clarence, Pete, Jim, May, Gladys]

JW: Oh they did? As cook or…?

BJ: Well they waited tables or whatever. Washed dishes.

JW: What year was that?

BJ: It was before '33.

JW: Okay. And that's Frank's daughters?

BJ: Yeah it was Frank's, my dad's half brother's daughters. Virginia's [Bill's wife's] grandmother. She cooked out at that camp.

JW: Oh really? What was her name?

BJ: Harpst.

JW: Harpst.

Traps

JW: How did the traps work, did you ever see one?

BJ: Oh, lots of them. They never went out until 1933.

JW: What did they look like?

BJ: I can show you a picture. There's one. That's just one fish trap. That's where they are brailing the fish.

JW: Brailing?

BJ: It's a net and they drop it down. It's got lead on each side of it and it holds it down, you know sinks it down. And then it's got floats up on the top that hold the things and when they drop it down it sinks and the fish get in it and then they use the boom on the boat and lift it up. They get a whole brail full of fish and they pick that up and swing it over the scow or the boat. It depends on what they're putting their fish in. If they've got scows, that's generally used up north, then you just bring it over there and give it a jerk and it would open up and the fish would drop in the hulls or in the scow or what ever it was.

JW: It would open up in the middle?

BJ: No, they would just drop it down see and then they would lift it up and the fish would just spill out of it.

JW: So you call it brailing.

BJ: There was two ways they could brail them. With a boat, with a brail on it. He's got a brail on the end of this. They drop that in there and it sinks. It's got lead weights on it. Then they get it full, they have a winch on it, they lift it up and dump the fish in the scow. See that's a scow load of fish.

JW: This one is Friday Harbor packing, What year do you think this was?

BJ: I would say that was in early 1900s.

PHOTO OF SCOW LOAD OF FISH - FHP Co. No. 1, Friday Harbor

PHOTO OF THE MICHIGAN BRAILING

BJ: The Michigan's the boat that Dad worked on when he learned how to get his mate's license.

JW: What kind of boat is it?

BJ: It was a cannery tender.

BJ: You see he's got his boom out. He's probably brailing the trap.

JW: And then he just swings it around?

BJ: He just pulls the boom up like that, swings it around and dumps it in the hull. They had a hull forward of the house and aft of the house. Those were pretty good-sized steamers.

JW: Yeah that's a good picture. Too bad it's fading. Okay this looks like it's called the Fair… This is just a… Is that a tug?

PHOTO FAIR… BOAT AND TRAP, SOUTH SIDE OF FINLAYSON

BJ: That's a cannery tender. See she's got one of these booms out too, they're brailing traps. Now I was trying to see where this might have been. I think Grandma's house was farther down this way.
JW: Is this flat or is it deeper?

BJ: It's flat bottom.

JW: You said that when you were a kid you remember that they had 60 men at least on those lifting places. That was the brailing lifting place?

BJ: Well they didn't brail so much in those days. They had pot scows. And they would take the scows right into the thing and then they had Spanish windlasses and they would keep lifting the net up.

JW: Spanish what?

BJ: Spanish windlasses.

JW: Windlasses?

BJ: Yeah.

JW: And that's like a…?

BJ: Well it was a round… They would get a round piece of wood, a trunk of a tree or something like that, it would probably be about that long, and they had long pieces of pipe or bars that went through it on each side. And two guys would get on that and they rope around it. And they would wind that rope around that and kept lifting the net up. And as they went along they would have to go up and tighten those windlasses up and lift the net up. They'd have it long enough so that the net would go as far down as they wanted. And then when they started getting the fish out they would just keep pulling that up and they would get the fish into the pot scows. They called them pot scows.

JW: Are there any pictures of that?

BJ: Well I haven't got any, no. I've seen it done so many times, and done it so many times, especially up north. But I wasn't very old when I saw it done. I would go with my dad. But it was 1933 and I wasn't but just out of high school. And I used to go with him on the boat. Heck even when I was six or seven years old. [1921-1922]

MAP OF MOSQUITO PASS SHOWS WINDLASS

PHOTO OF TRAP AND MEN ON TOP

BJ: That's a trap and these are all… See this is a pot scow. Let me see if I can find one of those wenches that I was talking about.

JW: What is this thing?

BJ: Well the guys are sitting up there. That's all that I know. I don't know what this net is doing in that either. But this is a pot scow and that's in the spiller where they're getting fish. But generally they had those Spanish windlasses that would keep lifting that net up. And I don't see any Spanish windlasses up there. But all the ones that I've ever been on, the traps, all of them in the later years, they always had those. And they had four of them and they would keep winding them up and bringing them up… And then they would bring the fish to the surface.

JW: And these are just little drift boats?

BJ: No that's what we called dories. And all of them were double-ended boats and all of the fish traps, that's what they used to go back and forth out to lift the traps.

JW: So where was this do you think?

BJ: Well I can't tell you just exactly where. It must have been down where the PAF traps were. It's on the Salmon Banks. When I was a kid there were so many, PAF in Bellingham had four traps stuck out, four of them. One after the other. They staggered them, like that. On the Salmon Banks.

PHOTO OF PAF TRAP, PAF Photo (Mitchell 1920)

JW: What's PAF?

BJ: Pacific American Fisheries.

PHOTO PAF Co. 44 DORIES AND LEAD

BJ: Henry Cayou had the trap right off of False Bay, just south of False Bay right on the first point there. He used to catch king salmon headed for the Fraser River. Sometimes he'd get 20 ton lifts. Just around the corner from False Bay there's a little island out in the middle of False Bay, right at the entrance. Just go around that corner and it's the first point to stick out. Kanaka Bay is just on the other side, just around the corner of the opening of False Bay.

Just a little bight south of False Bay, right there. That was all Fraser River king salmon. He used to get tons of them in that trap. He was a rich Indian.

This is the old Anderson place. And this is where Henry Cayou had his trap. That's the old Bill Oaks house. And this is where you go to Art Clements place, down this way.

MAP OF FALSE BAY TRAP LOCATION

JW: Did Henry Cayou live down there?

BJ: He was from Orcas. Henry Cayou. He had a boat called the Salmonaro.

JW: So he would come over on his boat.

BJ: Oh yeah.

JW: He operated the traps himself? Did he hire?

BJ: Oh he hired, sure. He had help. He had trap men and then he had lifting crew.

JW: So was he like his own company?

BJ: He owned that trap. He drove it and put it in.

JW: And then he would just sell to one of the packing operations.

BJ: I don't know who he sold to. Probably anybody that would buy it. That was king salmon and he could sell it to anybody that would want it.

JW: There was one cannery in Friday Harbor?

BJ: There was two originally. One went out of business. Later it became what they called the pea cannery. John Henry came over there from Mt. Vernon and started the pea cannery. They used to can; well they put up a hundred thousand or more cases of peas. San Juan Island peas. And they were good peas.

JW: Where was that located?

BJ: You know where the boat moorage is in town? It was right there.

JW: Where was the other cannery?

BJ: The other cannery was right there where the Friday Harbor Packing Company is.

PHOTO OF FRIDAY HARBOR PACKING COMPANY CANNERY AND *CITY OF ANACORTES*

JW: Right by the ferry terminal?

BJ: Just south of the ferry terminal. The ferry terminal is probably part of where dad used to park his boat.

JW: So they were pretty close to each other, the two canneries.

BJ: They were 150 yards apart, because the commercial dock was over…. It was the main ferry landing for years and years. That was there and the cannery was just on the other side of that.

JW: Jack McKenzie, who was he?

BJ: He owned the dock, the original dock where the ferry used to land. And they had a cannery down there and all the freight that came in came in over that dock.

JW: Tell me about the Salmon Bank, is it shallow there?

BJ: Fairly.

JW: And why is there so much salmon there.

BJ: Because that's the way the salmon come in up the strait through there. And there were rivers like the Skagit River and the river up by Bellingham, all along, creeks and things. A lot of the little things that we call creeks now, they were full of fish in the early days.

BATHYMETRY MAP from Ralph Haugerud, University of Washington

JW: The Salmon Bank is unique because it is shallow and they could put the traps there?

BJ: Yes. That was it. They could put the traps in.

JW: How many traps do you remember there at one time?

BJ: See there was San Juan Fishing, they had traps just on the other side of Eagle Point right across in here someplace. I don't know how many people had traps in there, any number. Years ago; there were traps… You would look from the school bus, look out there in the spring when they were driving piling and there would be pile drivers all along out there.

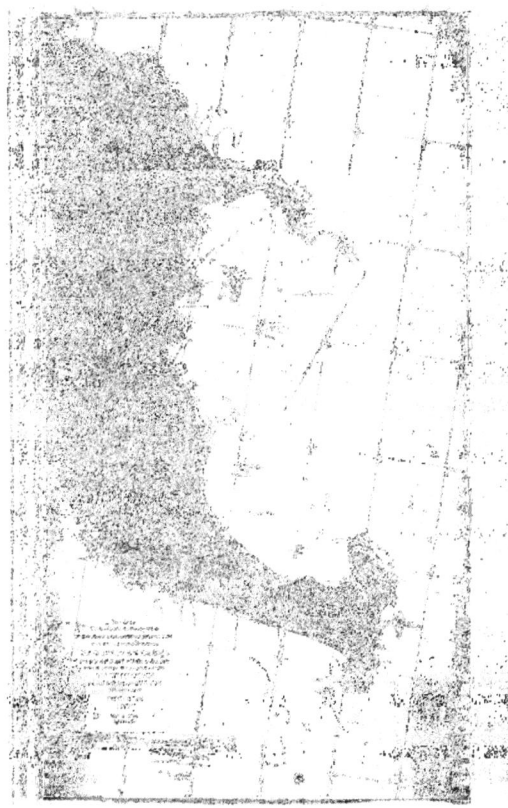

MAP OF TRAP LOCATIONS

JW: So all the way up were solid traps?

BJ: Well, I won't say solid traps. There's a certain amount of distance[9] because each of them had their own locations and that map that Jim's got shows you where they are and the name of them. Some of those must have went out there two and a half to three miles when they had all of the traps in there.

JW: That's amazing.

BJ: PAF had four traps. I've only seen that once in my lifetime. And they ran a Canadian steamer through it and after that they never allowed them to put the fourth trap in[10].

JW: Was it out too far?

---

[9] See regulations, end distance of 600 feet and lateral distance of 2400 feet between traps.

[10] In 1912 the US Corps of Engineers produced a series of maps depicting the presence of fish traps in the waters of Puget Sound and the Strait of Juan de Fuca to prevent mariners from becoming entangled in the leads (Radke 2002:75).

BJ: Yeah, it was too far out.

JW: That's the steamer that went aground?

BJ: No, no.

JW: Oh it's not?

BJ: No, no. It was way out halfway in the middle of the strait with four traps.

JW: See I was thinking that was the one that went aground.

BJ: No that was the… That was farther up the line, past False Bay, almost up to Lime Kiln Light, where that steamer went.

PHOTO OF STEAMER

JW: And what area do you call the Salmon Bank? This whole stretch?

BJ: Yeah, all along here.

BJ: Alaska Packers had one trap, Friday Harbor Packing Company had one trap, San Juan Fish Company had one trap, and PAF they had the three. A guy from Lopez, John Troxell had a trap closer to the pass going in [San Juan Channel]. And then like I say, Henry Cayou had a trap, they had a trap at Open Bay, they had traps right close to where the old lime kiln was.

JW: There was a trap there?

BJ: There were traps at Deadman's Bay.

MAP OF CATTLE POINT TRAP
MAP OF DEADMAN'S BAY, NO TRAP SHOWN

JW: Do you know, today it's called Granny's Cove south of Eagle Point, do you know that name? It was where the HBC used to land their little boats in the early days and there was a spring up on the hill there and an Indian house.

MAP OF GRANDMA'S COVE

PHOTO OF GRANDMA'S COVE

BJ: You know the only spring that was there was on the Alaska Packers site and we used to get, what is that, we used it for green's. And they got all their water for the cookhouse[11] and the men, unless something has happened to it, it used to be for years and years and years that my grandmother used to go down there and get…

JW: Her water?

BJ: Not her water, she had a good well.

JW: Greens?

BJ: She'd get those greens

JW: Watercress

BJ: Watercress.

---

[11] PAF acquired their water at the spring. PAF files include the following: "enclosed find check for $25. payable to Eliza Jakle in payment of rental for the water right at Salmon Banks camp"(PAF 1902). "I have seen Mrs. Jakles (sic) and presented the $25.00 check in payment for the water rent for 1902 to her. She refused to accept same until she had seen some other members of her family. Mrs. Jakles stated that in the conversation between herself and Mr. McMillan she told him that she would not take less than $50.00 a year and that she would not give a lease. Mrs. Jakles said that if the other members of the family did not object she was willing to take the $25.00, and that she would know today or tomorrow" (PAF 1902a). "This was my error pure and simple and I wish you would say to Mrs. Jakles for me that I am very sorry it occurred. When I asked Mr. McMillan what rent he had agreed upon he answered at once $50. but when he reported the matter to me I put down $25." (PAF 1902b).

PHOTO OF SPRING IN 2003, by Jacilee Wray

Indian fishing

JW: Back when Bryant and Jakle were doing this, it was the same type of operation?

BJ: Well, I can't tell you. They were doing it when I was big enough to see it. When it started, these big, like PAF out of Bellingham and Bellingham Canning, and Friday Harbor Packing Company, all the rest of them. It was big business in those days.

JW: Probably the peak?

BJ: Oh yeah.

JW: How did the Indians fish out here before the traps?

BJ: They fished the same old way as they still do, reef nets.

JW: Did those go into the ground too?

BJ: No, no

JW: It was just between boats.

BJ: Just between two boats.

JW: The state outlawed trap fishing, when?

BJ: Trap fishing, 1933.

JW: That was the end of it?

BJ: Yeah

JW: Did the Indians use the reef nets at the same time other people were trapping?

BJ: Oh yeah, heck yes.

JW: That was busy out there.

BJ: I worked on Open Bay, when I wasn't working at Roche Harbor, if I could get a chance on that I would get a job out there.

JW: Where's Open Bay?

MAP OF OPEN BAY

BJ: Do you know where Roche Harbor is, you turn the corner and you go down between Henry and down through that narrow pass. Just a bight on the end of Henry Island.

JW: So you worked on a reef net.

BJ: Yeah

JW: For any particular family?

BJ: No, well yeah, Wells. One of the Wells' brothers.

Packer Rock

BJ: This little point of land here, right off of here [packer rock]. If you had all of the lead that's lying on the bottom of the bay there you would have tons of it. They would hang up… There were rocks in there and the first thing when they came in there they would try to hook or drop off of there and then make their big circle. And they would get tangled up in those rocks. And I guess Dad said that if lead were a nickel a pound you would be a rich person.

JW: So they were anchors that ended up there?

BJ: No they were leads from the bottoms of the nets. They were lead balls with a hole through them that held the net down. Dad always told me that if they got all of the lead that was hung up on those rocks there they would have a fortune.

JW: Did you ever find lead when the tide went out?

BJ: No never. It was deep water. A stranger would come up here and hear about all the fish that were being caught around here and they didn't know about the rocks and they would set their nets and they would get tangled up in that rock pile and they would lose a lot of it.

JW: So it wasn't the fishing companies it was…

BJ: It was the fishermen themselves. Purse seiners. When I was fishing, when we had the traps we brailed all the fish out of the traps. If we bought them from the purse seiners then I sat there with five tally machines on a board and tallied them.

JW: And that's how they got paid for them? By the number of fish, not by the weight?

BJ: Then later years they started to weigh them. And you had to watch them like a hawk too.

JW: Would they take these barges around to Friday Harbor?

BJ: They towed the barges with a tugboat. He'd probably have his hull full of fish too.

JW: The tugboat was owned by the company as well?

BJ: Yeah.

JW: Did all the boats have names?

BJ: Yeah

JW: Did the barges have names?

BJ: Just numbers I think, at least I don't remember any names on them.

PHOTO OF WASHBURN GIRL

JW: Was this a post card or a picture that you took?

BJ: No that was a picture of a salmon that they caught in a trap at the Salmon Banks. This here is over in Friday Harbor. This was a post card of the Washburn girl.

JW: Oh, so you knew who she was?

BJ: Yeah. I went to school with her.

JW: Who took this?

BJ: I don't know who took it. It was a 108-pound King Salmon. That's an eleven-year-old girl. That's all that I can remember of it. I think that we've got an original picture of it at home.

JW: And this was from the Salmon Bank?

BJ: Yeah that's from the Salmon Banks.

PHOTO OF TRAP AT SALMON BANK

BJ: [Looking at photo of trap] It looks like they have a section of trap missing here. It looks like there's some piling out of a lead. But this one even looks like there's another trap going out beyond that. So that must be a PAF trap. And that's a pile driver in the background there. That was wire, galvanized wire on the leads. And a lot of the trap itself was wire. But the part that they lifted the fish out of, that was web. That was tarred web.

PHOTO FRIDAY HARBOR PACKING CO. TARRING NET

JW: So they put the net all the way around to follow these pilings? The tarred web followed all of these pilings?

BJ: No, that was wire. All of the leads were wire. And it was deep enough that they went clear to the bottom.

JW: So it held the outside of the net?

BJ: No it didn't have anything to do with it. It was just a line of piles that went out there and fish would hit that wire and they would follow it out until they would get into the traps. They had tunnels that went into the traps. And the fish would get in there, they would hit that and they would go in. And they would have a wing out here like this and they would get just like in a V and they would just keep going. Well they could swim through that tunnel and then they would get into the trap. Even part of the trap had wire in it. But the lifting part, the part in the pot, in the spiller, that was webbed.

See this is starting at the beach like this right here. And the traps are way out here at the end. And this is just a lead with the wire hanging down in the water. The fish come in along here in the shallower water and everything along here and they hit that lead. Well they can't go up the beach so they turn around and they start swimming out here. And like I say they have a tunnel that goes into the traps that guides the fish in there. And when they come to that tunnel, then they go right into the pot and the spiller. The lead goes from here on in to the beach. There's a net there so they can pick that... Keep pulling that net up.

JW: Okay, so they're bringing the fish in and the traps are all by the shore?

BJ: No the traps are out here. The lead just guides the fish into this. Into the pot and the spiller.

JW: This is where they drag them into?

BJ: They don't drag it in there; they just keep lifting that net up until... And then if they're brailing they have a brailing net there and they just drop that in there and get it full of fish and dump it either in the boat or in the scow.

DIAGRAM

JW: Okay. Quite an operation.

BJ: It was. That's the way that the people made their living in those days. San Juan Island was a fishing community. Everybody depended on the fishing fleet.

PHOTO OF MEN AND HOUSE, William Jakle, Sr., 2nd from right

JW: And this is just one of the houses down there?

BJ: That's part of where the lifting crews lived. In fact there's my dad I think. About the second one here from this end. I'm not sure, but it always looked like it was.

JW: Second from the right?

BJ: Right there.

BJ: Dad said he could remember when they had 60 men in the lifting crews. And later there were quite a few people who put traps in and never made a nickel out of them.

JW: Really?

BJ: In fact… one of my mother's aunts always hated dad over that because her husband put a trap in and he didn't make any money and he was not going to pay the guys any money for all of their summer work. And Dad put his foot down and said that he was either going to pay his crew off or he was going to get a licking. And the guy finally paid them off and Old Aunt Katie; she never forgave him for that.

MAP OF FISH CREEK

JW: So what was here at Fish Creek?

BJ: Fish Creek, everybody tied up their purse seiners down there in Fish Creek. We used a big scow out here for the purse seiners to mend their nets when they tore up their nets. And then all the rest of them held the fish. The big purse seiners and the smaller purse seiners and gill-netters would come up here as far as they could. And then the bigger purse seiners and things, they would tie up in here. This would be just jammed with boats.

JW: Is that privately owned today?

BJ: Must be.

JW: Was that part of your grandma's property?

BJ: That was part of it. After World War I; they finally gave her a deed. The Federal Government gave her a deed to it. How much of it I don't know.

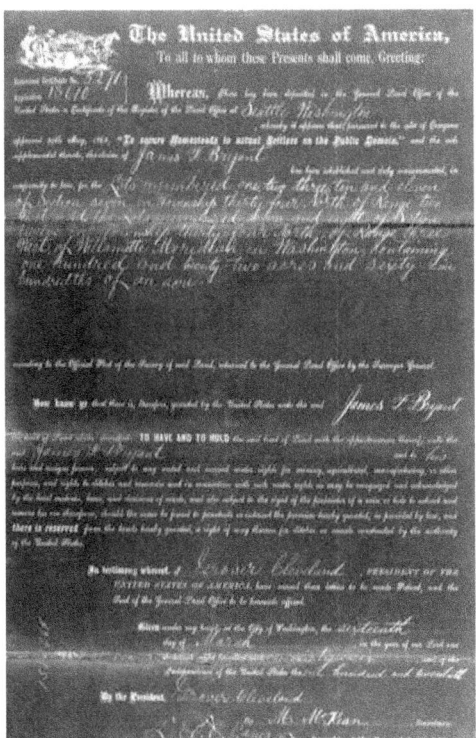

DEED FROM 1896

MAP SHOWING PROPERTY LISTED ON DEED

JW: PAF file says the scows and the pile drivers were drawn up on Warboss' land in the wintertime. Do you know where they drew up the scows and the pile drivers? Or did they take them somewhere else in the winter? You said they used to haul in the pilings down that way? [towards Old Town]

BJ: Quite a ways down farther.

JW: Oh okay. So would they pull them up here or would they pull them up to the shore where they were going to dump them?

BJ: Well they would pull them clear up back out of the water.

JW: How did they pull them? With horses?

BJ: No, no. They had steam pile drivers. We hauled the piles out and then piled them on the beach.

JW: So tell me again about where they got the pilings. About how they got the pilings.

BJ: Well they would find the trees the size that they needed and the length that they needed and they would fall them back in here [near Jakle's Lagoon]. Not all of them. They would find them other places too, but they harvested a lot. Grandma got a lot of money off of a lot of the trees in those days that she let them cut off of her land.

JW: Were they straight? Because a lot of these trees are kind of…

BJ: They were straight, real straight. They had to be real straight.

JW: And what kind of trees are they?

BJ: Fir trees.

JW: Douglas Fir?

BJ: Just fir trees. And then they would take the bark off of all of those trees. They would bark them.

Herring traps appear on inventory near South Beach in the 1930s (Appendix B)

JW: Do you remember them fishing off of Salmon Bank for Herring?

BJ: Not for herring.

JW: Not for herring?

BJ: No I never did.

JW: They must have just tried it and it wasn't a good spot or something.

BJ: Well there used to be lots of herring out there. You know we used to take, when we would go fishing… you know rowing just to catch a fish? The fish or something would get underneath and then we would get what we called a big herring ball. They would be right up on top and the seagulls would be after that by the hundreds.

JW: A herring ball?

BJ: Yeah. And the fish would get under the herring… It was just like the Orcas would bunch up the salmon. Well that's what the fish would do to the herring. They would feed on the herring.

JW: The salmon feed on the herring?

BJ: Oh yes. Right up in the gulf of Canada, you know just after you cross in that long gulf going up towards Cape Mudge they used to catch tons and tons of herring up in there. And they fished them so hard up there that they just spoiled their own salmon fishing. And it's the same thing that they did in Southeastern Alaska. When I first started going to Alaska, the women go up there and pack. In those days they had big fifty-gallon wood barrels and they would catch the herring and they would salt the herring. And the women would gut it you know. They would take the guts out of them. Herring chokers we used to call them.

JW: Why?

BJ: Well that's just what they did. That's all that they did.

JW: Chokers?

BJ: Well they took the insides, the guts out of them.

Looking at picture of purse seine boats in harbor

JW: Where are these houses at this point…?

BJ: That's between Ed McGeary and… down close to where Lizzie Lawson lived. This is False Bay and it had to be this way from False Bay. Maybe one of these places along here where these indents are.

PHOTO OF McGEARY BIGHT AND SAIL POWERED SEINE BOATS CIRCA 1910

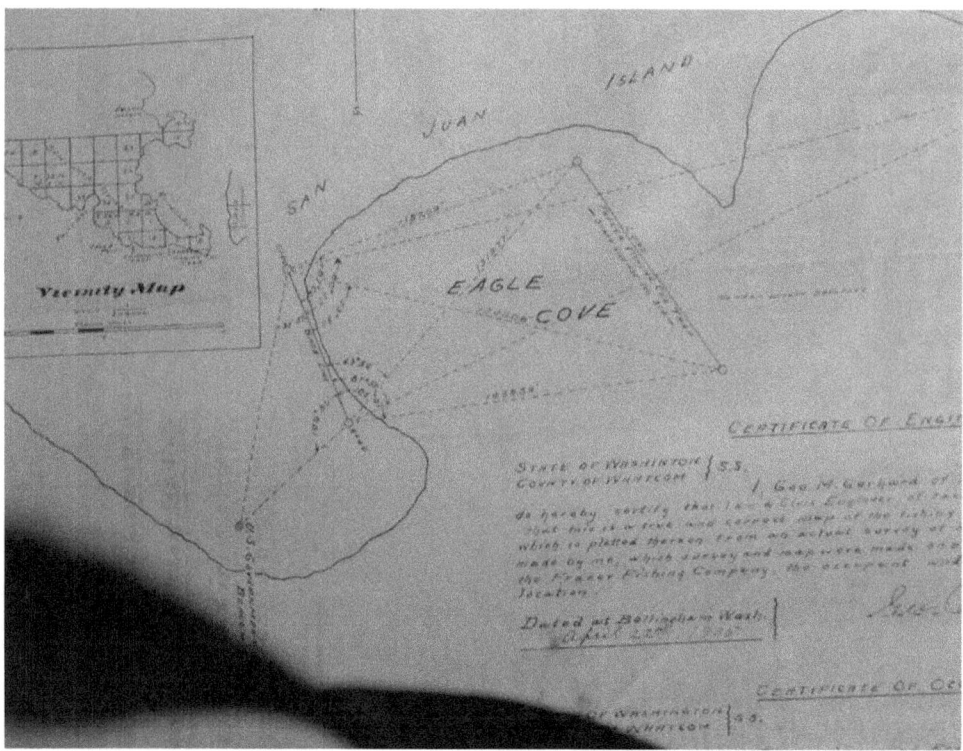

MAP OF THIS LOCATION

After traps banned

JW: So when the traps were outlawed, what changes did you see in the fishery? What did they do to compensate for that loss?

BJ: They got more purse seiners.

JW: More purse seiners?

BJ: More purse seiners and gill-netters.

JW: But that's a big investment right? Is that a bigger investment than traps?

BJ: Oh no. The trap would cost… They would work for weeks just driving the trap.

JW: To get it set up?

BJ: And then they had to hang the wire, and the nets all had to go in. And there was big, long pilings, all along those leads, to lash it together. Because if you put a pile by itself and the tide and the waves on it, pretty soon they would pop up.

JW: What's "original two pile dolphin"? [From PAF notes]

BJ: That's what they were, two piles.

JW: Why do they call it dolphin?

BJ: Well that's just been a name that's all… When you drove a couple of piles like that and used them to moor boats or scows or something to. They've always been called dolphins.

MAP WITH CLUMP OF PILES

JW: You know one thing, I don't know where it is, I didn't see it, but your dad, William Jakle, had a trap. His name was associated with a trap; did you know that he had two traps? [William Jakle and William Shultz[12], 7/28/1911 (2635 &2636)]

BJ: No. He probably did but I…

Canning

BJ: Sockeye was the biggest run in the spring, or the earliest, you know. But every kind of fish came, every kind of fish. But the sockeye was the main moneymaker. And on these traps they destroyed so much young fish. Tons and tons of it. They would get salmon trout [smolt?] you know that was too small to can or anything so when they lifted the traps they just dumped them into the pot scow and they would take them in and just pool out the fish that was big enough to can. And the rest of it they would just hook onto the pot scow and hoist it up in the air and dump all the rest of them out and they were dead you know.

JW: So did you eat a lot of fresh salmon, every night?

BJ: No, not every night. No, no. But we had all of the salmon that we ever wanted to eat. For years and years.

JW: Kanaka Bay Road.

BJ: Yeah. Kanaka Bay. He used to have a store there for fishermen's stuff. And he had a buyer laying there to collect fish.

JW: Where did Henry Cayou take the salmon?

BJ: To the canneries.

JW: Just in Friday Harbor?

BJ: Well wherever he could sell them.

JW: It seems like you said that there was a fish buying boat out there too?

BJ: Oh lots of them. PAF had them there. The San Juan Fish Company had them. The Friday Harbor Packing Company had them. Every fish-canning outfit in Puget Sound had buyers there.

JW: Was that the best place around for getting fish?

BJ: That was… In my days and my dad's days that was the fish… Between that and Whidbey Island. From where the naval station is along that high bank, clear down to the other end they used to have fish traps all along that too on Whidbey Island.

JW: Oh they did?

BJ: I used to buy fish for years.

JW: That's right. In Alaska didn't you?

BJ: In the Puget Sound too. All over the Puget Sound. I used to run the Neah Bay; I used to run up the Whidbey Island and all over Puget Sound.

---

[12] Shultz was Friday Harbor Packing Company Superintendent.

References

PAF Correspondence, Box 15/ Washington State Archives, Northwest Region

        1901   To Thomas Hudson, Fairhaven, From James Burke, June 5, 1901

        1901a To Thomas Hudson, Fairhaven, From James Burke, July 3, 1901

        1902   To James Burke, From Thomas Hudson, January 16, 1902.

        1902a   To Thomas. Hudson, From James Burke, January 20, 1902,

        1902b To James Burke, From Thomas Hudson, January 21, 1902

Etta Egeland Interview:
"To me it's naturally Salmon Banks"

The following are excerpts from two interviews with Etta Egeland; July 2, 2001 and September 26, 2001.

EE: Yeah. That's called Salmon Banks Beach right through the years. And at that time they used horses to pull the fish in because they would have these nets that were rolled up at… They were in a dory. That's a dory boat. That's a rowboat. But it's a different type of rowboat. It's more rounded, the bottom is more rounded. And they would have these nets and they would take them in the dory and go out when the fish were coming in. Go out and circle around the fish. And then they would come back in and they'd have their quantity of fish you know.

JW: Who were the fisher people? Who was fishing?

EE: The people that I'm speaking of were my family. My aunt [Lizzie] and my mother. In my mother's family there were eight children, four girls and four boys. So that way she had sisters that she grew up with. And the family always, all through their lives they were very close to one another. I can't remember them ever having disagreements. They just accepted each person in the family for what they were. And didn't bother about any little difference in opinion. They accepted them as they were.

PHOTO OF LIZZIE LAWSON SITTING TO THE LEFT OF BILL JAKLE, SR.

JW: Did just the men fish? Or did the women fish too?

EE: That's what I'm speaking of now. They'd take these dories and they would go out with the fish net when the fish were coming in. See the fish came in… The fish weren't always there and they would circle around a bunch of fish. And there was lots of fish.

JW: Did the women do this? Did your mom fish?

EE: Well I don't recall her fishing but she was right there and she may have been at times when the men weren't around and they had to row in the dory that took the net and went around the fish as the fish were coming in to the area[13].

JW: Did they sell the fish?

EE: I don't ever remember them selling the fish.

JW: So it was probably for home use? They would prepare it?

EE: Oh yes they salted fish. And smoked fish.

JW: And this was all different kinds of salmon or do you remember any particular kind?

EE: Well the first salmon that come through are humpbacks. [Actually, the first would be the sockeye. They can run through the humpback season, from July and August, into fall] And then you have the sockeye, they come next. Well the humpbacks are a different texture. And they have more oil in them. They're fatter than the fish that come second. What did I say?

JW: Sockeye.

EE: Sockeye. They [humpback] had more fat on them than the sockeye. The sockeye were a much lighter fish.

JW: How old were you when they did this type of fishing?

EE: When we were down there?

JW: Yeah, how old do you think you were?

EE: I would say that I possibly was... Because I was at my aunt's, living there with my aunt since I was... In 1900 I was six years old, so I was perhaps seven or eight years old.

JW: Now where did your aunt live? Did she live on the homestead too?

EE: Yes, when her father [Peter Larson] decided that he no longer could work his farm you know, and so he sold the forty to my aunt. And I'm not sure, this could always be left out, but I think his property had two forties of waterfront. And he sold her possibly one forty. And I imagine that... See this property was homesteaded. You went to Olympia and got your patent out to have the property. And I would guess that he had two forties of waterfront when he got through. And two forties in the back. So that way he had eighty...

JW: A hundred and sixty acres.

MAP OF PETER LARSON PLACE

EE: ... Berg I think that was...

JW: Berg?

EE: Her father [John Berg] worked on a fish trap later. But of course at first there wasn't such. The fish were hauled in as I mentioned earlier by a rowboat and pulled in by force.

JW: When did they put the fish traps in? Do you remember?

---

[13] Etta must have meant she did not fish commercially, as the following quote is from a 1990 oral history publication. "My mother loved to fish. She loved to go out and spend a day fishing just to get away.... Once I rowed the boat for her when she went fishing. Fishing never appealed to me after that. I am not a boat person" (Strickland 1990:49).

EE: No I don't remember. There was… I remember three fish traps.

JW: Where at?

EE: Right down on the Salmon Banks Beach.

JW: All three right in a row?

EE: Yes.

JW: And who operated those?

EE: I wouldn't be surprised that there were different people that had put those fish traps in. Because I don't know why one person would put more than one trap in.

JW: Right.

EE: And there was fish enough for everybody. Because there was lots of fish when they started. Humpbacks and sockeye.

JW: What about clams? Did you ever go clam digging?

EE: They went clam digging in front of my aunt's and her father's homestead down by… There was… Well it was quite a good beach with a lot of pebbles on it. But on the west end there was a jut out from it that had a lot of rocks and low land on the rocks, and it was connected with the island. The bay came to the edge of it and then it jutted out and the salt water was around the end of it. It came in. And the other side had the nicest beach on it. And that was a good place to find agates.

JW: Really.

EE: We got a hundred agates down there. I have different jars of agates that were picked up on what they call South Beach.

JW: South Beach.

EE: To me it's naturally Salmon Banks.

JW: Do you know what kind of clams they got in front of their place?

EE: Well I can't say that I know much difference about clams. There were different types of clams. There was a clam that had a very blue scalp and it was a different shape, but not many of them. But the regular clam was in the area.

JW: Like this big?

EE: Yeah.

JW: Butterclams maybe?

EE: Yeah they were good sized.

JW: Did you ever try octopus?

EE: Octopus? Yes. Down in that swamp area where the land extended out from the beach. There was the first octopus that I think that I ever looked at. And there were some Indian children who had come in there. The

Indians lived on the island. They came to the island. And I've forgotten the name of the place that they really settled down like going home. But they spent a lot of time on that beach down there.

References

Strickland, Ron
 1990 Whistlepunks and Geoducks: Oral Histories from the Pacific Northwest. Oregon State University Press, Corvallis

Interview with Bill Mason and Babe M. Jewett
"That's what they call the Salmon Bank"

The following are excerpts from an interview with Bill Mason and Babe M. Jewett on September 25, 2001, with Mike Vouri.

BM: There's a buoy a mile and a half southwest of Cattle Point. Well there's a bank that runs from the… Oh about three miles, no not that far. A mile, well maybe two miles from Cattle Point, runs out to that buoy. And none of that water is over ten fathoms deep. And that's what they call the Salmon Bank. And on those charts it's listed as the Salmon Bank. And we always used to call that the Salmon Bank Beach. Well when they put that road in there the county commissioner on the island here was a good friend of mine. And I used to tell him, Carl have that sign changed. That isn't South Beach that's Salmon Bank Beach. Okay I'll take care of it. I was after him again. I was after him at least four or five times. He never did have it changed. He wouldn't. I don't know whether it was too much to put on one of those signs about that long, Salmon Bank Beach, or what his deal was. But there used to be a road. Well I can show you where it went. It wasn't from Salmon Bank Beach, or it wasn't South Beach. Let's see where is it now? Where is South Beach?

MV: Where the shading is on the bottom of the hill.

BM: Oh, right here, yeah. And it shows it going down here. But the road, that wasn't there. This was when I tried to get them to change the name. And the road was down here like this where people went down there in that big… Well right on Eagle Point there was… Just before Eagle Point there was a little point there and that was called the Alaska Packers trap location, and there was a lead there. Believe it or not you could walk on the beach and they had piling about every fifteen feet. And they had a wire up about three and a half feet high that you could hold onto and then a log that was cabled onto the piling that was driven into the ground. You could walk clear to the trap and then walk out there and see the fish living in the trap.

MV: Is that from that big rock down there?

BM: Exactly.

MV: So that's why they call that Alaska Packer's Rock.

BM: Right exactly.

MV: So there was a fish trap off of the end of the rock and you could actually walk out to the fish trap?

BJ: Well, yes and the guys lived on the beach and they could go back and forth.

BM: And there were two or three along out here along that bank. Where that shallow water is. And that was the Pacific American Fisheries location.

JW: So these weren't Indian fish traps these were company fish traps?

BM: Yeah they were… The only Indian fish trap that I know of was the one at False Bay. There was one right off of this point here. And that was… His name was Henry Cayou.

BM: If the light is right here on the very point, and this goes out here and there's another light here and this is all ten fathoms or less, minus five. And let's see this would be… Well that's kind of a misnomer, but this would be Eagle Point and right here there's a little bay with a rock and it's pretty shallow this way. That little bay is called Old Camp. Because in the old days they didn't have any living quarters on their boats. And in the very early beginnings they rode from Eagle Harbor and Port Townsend to here and they camped in Old Camp, which would be about here.

PHOTOS OF McGEARY BIGHT (Eagle Cove) FROM WHATCOM COUNTY MUSEUM

JW: So there was good moorage there?

BM: Yeah, pretty good moorage there unless the wind blew too hard. And they camped a lot in Kanaka Bay too. I've been to Kanaka Bay when I've seen fifty, sixty, seventy purse seiners in there anchored.

JW: How deep does that get when the tide's in?

BM: Well, parts of it are very shallow and rocky and there are other parts that are quite deep for minus tides and everything.

JW: Were there ever any fish traps out at lime kiln that you remember?

BM: No there were none there, but there was one at Deadmans Bay.

JW: Oh where the county park is right?

BJ: No. Deadmans Bay.

JW: This is Small Pox.

BM: Yeah. This is Deadmans Bay and there was one here. And that was called the Lowman Trap Location.

JW: Lowman?

BM: Yeah, Lowman. I don't know. See the traps were taken out in 1932-I think.

BJ: Before you got out of school. Before you got out of high school

BM: See this lead was here to here. It was wire nailed on those posts clear to the bottom and so the fish would come up against that and it led them right in… And then into one pot, what they called a pot. And then another led into another one. I think it was three and the last was called a spiller and that's where they got in there and brailed the fish into little pot scows.

Interview with Bill Chevalier and Fran Chevalier
"Fishermen are becoming an endangered species"

The following are excerpts from an interview with Bill and Fran Chevalier on September 26, 2001

BC: Back in those days there was no Customs. Even when I was in my teens [1940s]. I started fishing up at Stuart Island on my grandfather's reef nets and the Indians would paddle over in their canoes from Canada and camp on the beach and fish over here and then they would go back over across the line. And there was nothing said. And they would come over here and I can remember canoes… These Indians, there would be about two or three of them in a fairly good-sized canoe and they would come over and fish lingcod.

JW: By Stuart?

BC: Yes, up around Stuart Island, Reid Harbor, Spieden Island and around Roche Harbor and Henry Island. The Indians would camp on the beaches and they would travel back and forth. Years ago they thought because they lived around Mitchell Bay, they were a tribe. Maybe that is why the Mitchell Bay Tribe is not recognized.

JW: Right. So maybe it was different people from different areas?

BC: I think that it was just a group of people that lived in Mitchell Bay.

BC: But Grandpa Edward Graignic was looking for a place to beach seine herring. And he went through the islands and he came across…

JW: So there was a market for herring at that time? A big market for herring?

BC: Well he had some kind of a curing recipe that he had in France and he started a little cannery up on Waldron. He smoked these herring, cured them I should say. And then they'd take his product to Vancouver, Bellingham, Victoria, and sell them. And that's how he made his money.

JW: Okay. Your grandma and grandfather, Lena and Edward had how many kids?

BC: Frank, Prosper, and Peter Graignic. Those were the three boys. And then there was Louise, Marie – Aunt Marie, Elizabeth [Bill's mom]

JW: So how did you take up fishing? You were obviously brought up around fishing…?

BC: Well let's see. It must have been about in 1940 because I was about eleven or twelve years old I think when I first started fishing. And of course grandpa had the reef nets. My cousin and I are about the same age and he would say okay you kids get out there and go fishing. I'll give you a half a share apiece. Well gee whiz we went out and worked our tails off. You know in those days there were a lot of fish.

JW: How do you reef net? Do you sit there and wait?

BC: Yes.

JW: And then you see the school?

BC: It's two boats side by side like this and they have leads. The tide has to come through these leads and through the boats, where the net is between the two boats. And then you have these poles. They're like ladders on one end and they look down in the water and they see the fish coming in.

JW: Are you kind of sitting up high?

BC: Yes, and then when they come over the front of the net why they pull it up. See that's the old Indian…[way]

BC: In 1983 I bought the seiner, that one right above the TV there. That's my boat.

JW: What's it called?

BC: The *Intruder*. And that was this year, our one-day of fishing.

JW: I heard it was a good year though.

BC: That day right there I had her plugged full of fish. Couldn't get anymore.

JW: You haven't had a year like that in a long time though.

BC: No. And that's right off of Stuart Island.

JW: Is it?

BC: Yes, right over the bow there, that's the entrance going into Reid Harbor on the left-hand side. And that's where the reef nets are.

JW: And are there still reef nets out there?

BC: Yep. I think Charlie just took them in. I've heard that he picked up the gears and took them in for the season.

JW: So they're owned… Is the location owned?

BC: Yes. It's registered with the state. See there's certain little areas designated on the chart. You can buy a license for gear for this certain area. Like Stuart Island, I think that there are two or three reef net sites there that are legal for Stuart Island. And of course Lummi Island, they have… I don't know how many are up there. There's probably fifteen of twenty reef nets up there in that area. Then over here on Shaw Island by Flat Point. Between Flat Point and Fisherman's Bay there are a couple of sites that are designated. (See RCW in binder under regulations)

JW: Now Charlie is your…?

BC: Cousin. That was Alfred's. [Ed and Mary Chevalier's son Alfred married Adeline and their son is this Alfred]. They were lost up in Alaska and I can't remember what year that was. But they were on a crab boat. Well they were fishing crab, but they were asphyxiated. And then the boat went down and they couldn't find them for about two weeks. But they finally located the boat.

JW: So who fishes with you? Are your kids part of your crew?

BC: Oh Yes, I have three sons.

JW: And they all fish with you?

BC: Yep. Matthew, Marty and Mitchell. And of course this year the kid that's in the skiff there he's my grandson. He's eighteen and he was there. He kind of took my place for jumping around you know.

JW: And a license. Nobody can get a license anymore; you just have to inherit them, right?

BC: Yes. Of course I'm Indian see. I'm 3/8 Indian.

JW: So do you not need a license?

BC: No. No I fish under the Swinomish Tribe.

JW: But they only have a limited number?

BC: Well of course the tribe limits how many boats there are, but there aren't that many boats anymore because they just can't make it and they lose them.

JW: If a license is handed down like property, is your right to fish handed down like property as well?

BC: No.

JW: No, so your kids could all be independent fishermen?

BC: Yes. They took our kids in as associate members. Their bloodline is only three sixteenth and mine is three eighths. I only have a quarter for Swinomish. No, it may only be one eighth I guess. Yes it would be one eighth and the bloodline is set at a quarter to get your rights to fish. I told them at the tribe, I said pretty soon there's not going to be any bloodline, eventually. Because they marry out of the tribe.

JW: There's only a few more generations.

BC: Yes. Right now there are a lot of them over there that are only a sixteenth or even less.

JW: So where are some of the prime spots on the island? I remember one year we came out and we kayaked out off of the beach by American Camp. I guess the Salmon Bank area. And that's always a place where you see a lot of fishing boats.

BC: Oh Yes.

JW: But do you have a favorite area around here or do you just try your luck? Or is that top secret?

BC: No. No as a matter of fact I was... Well, Charlie Chevalier has a purse seiner too, just like mine. And there was only I think about four of us out there. We start in at different stages of the tide, but we start in on the Salmon Banks. The old trap site. You know as the road goes down to the beach there. It's just on the right hand side. Well that's the old trap.

JW: Is that Alaska Packers?

BC: Yes.

JW: Okay.

BC: Yes and then of course Eagle Point, Pile Point and the lime kiln and up off of the park [Smallpox Bay], and Mitchell Bay and up at Stuart Island. Well I had about I think six thousand or something there off of the park, San Juan Park. And then I ran up to Stuart Island and had about another six thousand.

JW: What kind?

BC: Sockeye.

JW: What month was that for sockeye?

BC: That was the 30th of July. Yep. And I mean there was just all kinds of fish. You know there was only a run size of, I forget what it was, five million or something. And they wanted three million per escapement. And of course the Americans and the Canadians have to divide the catch. And then the Indians get part and it's a mixed up mess. But anyway there were fish going through here from the 18th of June till almost the 1st of September.

JW: Why do you think there were so many this year?

BC: Well, I think the water temperature has changed.

JW: Warmer?

BC: El Nino has disappeared.

JW: Colder then?

BC: Yes it's colder. Colder water. And before, when El Nino was out here we'd get mackerel out on the Salmon Banks and that's a warm water fish, or warmer water. I mean you know they come up from California or something. Well there was mackerel out here. So the biggest percentage of the fish used to go through Johnstone Straits between Vancouver Island and the mainland in Canada.

JW: Oh.

BC: You know the passage you just go down through Georgia Strait and then into the Fraser River. But this year there was about eighty percent that came through Haro Strait and Juan de Fuca Strait. I'm pretty sure that it was just that the water temperature was down. My theory is that maybe they follow what we used to call the Japanese current. And now it's El Nino and La Nina and I think they more or less follow the edge of that warm water. And it just happened that they came down this way. And of course they know where to go.

JW: So where do you take your fish? Where's the buyer?

BC: Well the buyer is out of Bellingham. I have my own buyer that comes and follows me around. Because I've had... I mean I'm not bragging but I do pretty good fishing. I'm just about high boat every year. Anyway, I like to have a buyer come right up along side of me, right there you see -- between the seine skiff and the big boat there's this great big bag of fish and we have to brail them. What we call brail. It's just like a dip net, salmon dip net that you put down. Of course it's good size and it takes about two hundred fish at a whack. We have to lift it up and swing it over and you have a little string and they pull it and it opens up the bottom of this bag and the fish drop down into the fish hole. I like to have a buyer follow me around that has a pump. It's a 12-inch pump that they just put down in the water, suck the fish right out.

JW: And then you can get out there and get some more quickly.

BC: Yes. It gives me a chance to go fishing. I don't weigh the fish. They put them down the hole and they're in chilled water. And just like this year they said, oh my gosh, there were fish still swimming in the boat when they unloaded them in Bellingham the next day.

JW: Well I sure didn't see any of those in our grocery store this year. All they had was Atlantic farm salmon.

BC: Oh. I hope you didn't buy any.

JW: No, I refuse.

BC: Oh no. Boy you know they feed them those pellets.

JW: But where do the fresh sockeye go?

BC: Well they go up into the Fraser River.

JW: No, I mean the market? Where do they take them?

BC: I don't know so much anymore. Most of them go to Japan. Or they used to. But they told me that there are a lot of them going to... I think France. They freeze them whole. There's about fifteen to twenty I think in a block of ice and then they put plastic around this block and shove it in a cardboard box and close it up and put it in a freezer and that's how they keep them. And of course there are buyers. They have these cells. And they have fish brokers who sell them all over. But it's all right for restaurants back east and the Midwest to call and say I want three hundred pounds of salmon. And of course these fish farms can go dip them out and send them back there the year round. But the natural stock they can't do that. I mean it's a seasonal thing and they've got to freeze them or have someway to keep them. So the market now is probably almost fifty-percent farm raised salmon.

FC: When Bill was fishing we would go to Eagle Cove and take the kids. The girls took the kids to the beach and we sunbathed. It was Eagle Point. Eagle Cove. Because the other beach, Long Beach wasn't open yet. That was still privately owned and locked up wasn't it?

JW: Is Long Beach, South Beach in the park? Now some fish packing company owned that for a long time didn't they?

BC: Well Kenny Dougherty owned the property out there. But Whiz Fish Company put the dock in at Fish Creek. And there was a gate… Well you know just about where the road is going down to Long Beach… Well there was a house down below that.

FC: A big barn.

BC: And there was just like an old wagon trail I guess that used to go in there and come out at Fish Creek. And there was a gate across there that we used to have the key to. If you fished for the fish company why you could get a key to get out to Fish Creek. The people from Friday Harbor that fished for Whiz Fish Company, why they could get a key and go out and drive out and we could keep our boats out there at Fish Creek.

PHOTO OF 4-WHEEL BUGGY ON ROAD TO FISH CREEK

JW: And it's Whiz?

BC: Yep. Whiz. There was New England Fish Company, Washington Fish and Oysters and well there were a bunch of them out there.

JW: And they owned trap sites at one time I understand out there.

BC: Yes, I think it was APA that had the traps. There was a trap right at the end of Long Beach. And there was a trap at False Bay and there was one at Mitchell Bay. There was one at Stuart Island. Boy, there were traps all over. They had even trapped up to Waldron at one time.

Appendix A

Trap Inventory at or near the Salmon Banks

Date	Name	Lic. #	Town	Loc.	Misc.
04/26/99	AP Co.	620		Salmon Bank	West side
06/08/99	A.V. Reeves	1252		Salmon Bank	East edge
1900	Sweeney	145		Salmon Bank	
1900	PAF	1224		Salmon Bank	
1900	PAF	46/47	/48/49	Salmon Bank	
1900	PAF	4		Salmon Bank	
1900	AP Co.	1788		Salmon Bank	
1900	PAF	2253		Salmon Bank	
1900	A & D	1633		Salmon Bank	
1900	AP Co.	620		Salmon Bank	West side
1901	APA	643		Eagle Point	
1901	A & D	200		Eagle Point	
1901	A & D	295			
1901	A & D	1548/	1549	Salmon Bank	
1901		7953		Near pass	
1901	A & D	1549		Salmon Bank	
1901		1051		Salmon Bank	Not Fished
1901		98		Salmon Bank	Fished
04/05/05	Alexander & Bullock	47	Blaine	South SJ	
04/14/05	Dolphin Fishing Co.	1654	B'ham	South SJ	
04/14/05	Lion Fishing Co.	400	B'ham	South SJ	Lot 4
05/05/05	Frazer Fishing Co.	314	B'ham	Eagle Cove	Sec 7
05/06/05 [Renewed 03/05/06 new 2012]	Will A. Lowman	220	Anacortes	South SJ	
05/16/05 [Transferred from J.S. Woodlin, Anacortes 04/22/05]	Will Lowman	776	Anacortes	South SJ	Lot 11
06/03/05	Lummi Is Fishing Co	1760	Anacortes	South SJ	Lot 4/6
06/03/05	Longhorn	2413		W SJ	
06/05/05	Dolphin Fishing Co.	1654		South SJ	Lot 6
06/05/05.	Lion Fishing Co	488	B'ham	South SJ	Lot 4
06/07/05	Turner, Lester	2044		East SJ	Kanaka Bay
06/07/05	Salmon Bank Fish Co.	104/	105	East SJ	
06/07/05	Mosquito Pass	2220	B'ham	West SJ	
06/07/05 [Abandoned 05/08/33 Trap No. 1]	Mosquito Pass	2531		South SJ	Sec 12/7
07/06/05	Lowman, Will	2388	Anacortes	Kanaka Bay	
07/08/05	Cornelieas Coghlan	806		Deadmans Bay	
11/27/05	Robert A. Smith	2336	B'ham	East SJ	
04/04/06	Pringle, J.C.	764	PT	South SJ	
12/05/06	Lummi Is. Fishing Co.	606		South SJ	
05/08/08	Coast Fish Co.	404	Anacortes	Kanaka Bay	Abd 8/17/16

Date	Name	Lic. #	Town	Loc.	Misc.
04/07/10	Mitchell Bay Fish Co.	408		Mitchell Bay	
[Renewed 04/01/12 & Renewed 04/01/15]					
07/28/11	Shultz & Jakle	2635/	2636	South SJ	
02/20/12	Thos. Smith	412		Mitchell Bay	Abd. 1916
03/11/12	Cayou and Haroldson	4040		SW SJ	
11/21/12	Emery Graham	3982	Anacortes	West SJ	
		3999			
		4065			
		4066			
		4067			
03/25/13	Edw. Daugherty	4119	FH	South SJ	
[Assigned to SJ Fishing and Packing 02/11/16 became 569]					
07/05/13	Lion Fishing Co.	2335	B'ham	Cattle Point	
[Abandoned]					
01/30/14	S.A. Hall	3640	B'ham	SJ Is	
04/03/14	Haro Fish Co.	466	B'ham	West SJ	
		465			
02/19/15	Geo Fisher	3626	B'ham	South SJ	
[Transferred to Cypress Fish Co. 06/1917 became 211]					
04/01/15	Peter Gragnic	378	PT	Andrews Bay	
04/01/15	Peter Gragnic	369		Open Bay, Henry Is	
04/01/15	Katherine Fisher	152	B'ham	South SJ	
04/08/15	John Peterson	----	FH	South SJ	
04/14/15	D. Campbell	146		Iceberg Pt	
08/30/16	Geo C Fisher/ J M McCue	----	B'ham	Eagle Point	
04/01/16	Henry Cayou	377	Deer Hrbr	South SJ	34N3W Sec4
06/05/16	Henry Cayou/ Haroldson	259	Deer Hrbr	South SJ	Sec 33/34
02/08/17	F.H. Packing	5095		S. Cattle Pt.	
04/02/17	J.K. McKenzie/ Chas. Thacker	1617		Low Pt., Griffin Bay	
04/30/17	Fisher/McCue	2620	B'ham	S. Cattle Pt.	
06/04/17	John Troxell	3382	Richardson	Cattle Point	
[Abandoned 08/25/17]					
03/11/17	Cascade Packing Co.	6716		SJ Pass, Cattle Pt.	
	Cascade Packing Co.	6715	Anacortes	S SJ Pass, Lopez	
12/19/18	Cayou	6404		False Bay	
02/25/19	San Juan Canning Co.	501		W SJ	
08/29/19	Emerson Lightheart	5925		W SJ near Mitchell Bay	
10/21/19	Robert Flynn	6888	FH	West SJ	

Date	Name	Lic. #	Town	Loc.	Misc.
12/30/19	Ahston Gross	7310	FH	West SJ	
12/31/19	S.B. Gross	7311	FH	West SJ	
04/12/21	W.A. Clement	1502	FH	SW SJ	
05/12/21	Booth Fisheries	445	Seattle	West SJ	
09/24/23 [Cancelled 9/15/22]	H.J. Cayou	4493		Kanaka Bay	SE point [Pound net]
11/07/23	Will Lowman	4402		South SJ	
08/27/24	Will Lowman	4263		Kanaka Bay	Pile Pt.
07/18/25	C.J. Benglann, Pres. Am. Floating Fish Trap Co.	4560	Seattle	Kanaka Bay	N Shore [Floating trap]
10/07/25	Emmett Coughlan	5719	FH	Deadmans Bay	[Pound net]
11/20/25	Nooksak Canning Co.	6015	Everett	Cattle Point	[Pound net]
1926 [Renewed 1928 and 04/07/1931]	Eunice Troxell	315		Smallpox Bay	
07/24/26	D.W. Wood	4894, 4895		Westcott Bay	[Brush weir]
10/14/27 [Amended 04/03/34 changed #203]	Catherine Coughlan	7662		Deadmans & False Bay	
03/17/29	H.J. Cayou	752		South SJ	False Bay [Pound net]
06/25/28	W.R. Morgan	4895		Westcott Bay	[Brush weir]
09/22/28	Wm. Griswold	7925	B'ham	Cattle Point	[Pound net]
09/24/28 [Abandoned 09/24/28]	H J Cayou	6539		False Bay and Kanaka Bay	
01/26/29	John Troxell	8883		South SJ	
02/28/29	C.E. Alexander, JF Olinder, EE Murray	9031		N. Kanaka	Abd. 3/18/29
03/06/29	H.J. Cayou	6539		West SJ	
05/17/29	Catherine Coughlan	1744		Deadmans & False Bays	
03/18/29	C.E. Alexander	9031	Seattle	West SJ	
07/23/29	Wm. Norton	7462	Deer Hrbr	SW SJ	
11/27/29	Astoria & P. S. Canning Co.	421	B'ham	W SJ	
02/05/30	Cayou	5476		W SJ	
11/24/30 [Abandoned 01/19/31]	Frank Martinis	9504	Anacortes	SW SJ	T34NR3W Sec. 3/Lot 5
05/11/32	Catherine Coughlan	324		West SJ	
09/1932 [Abandoned 11/25/32, 7448 Abandoned 01/11/33]	Cayou	7218, 580, 7448		S SJ	

Date	Name	Lic. #	Town	Loc.	Misc.
05/08/33	Mosquito Pass Fish Co.	4046	B'ham	S SJ	
05/08/33	Salmon Bank Fish Co.	4002 4003		S SJ	
[Abandoned 03/14/34, 4046/4002 and 4003 listed on map as Salmon Bank Fish Co.]					
05/08/33	PAF	517		S SJ	
[Abandoned 03/14/34, conveyed to PAF 06/08/34 by #28390]					
06/27/33	H.B. Murray	---		Deadmans Bay	
07/26/33	Salmon Bank Fish Co.	5554 5555	B'ham	Salmon Bank	
[Abandoned 03/14/34, conveyed to PAF 06/08/34 by 28390]					
01/09/34	A.J. Martini	6888	W SJ		
03/04/34	PAF	7216 7217 7218 7219 541		Salmon Bank	Sec 12/7
06/20/34	B W Huntoon [PAF]	261		Cattle Point	Sec 7
	Seafood Investments	3351		Cattle Point	Sec 12 [Brush weir]
04/19/35	A W Deming	3329 3330 3331		Cattle Pt.	 [Herring/ brush weir]
05/23/38	Raymond Robinson	6111	Anacortes	Eagle Point & Cattle Point [Beach seine]	
04/01/39	Seafood Investment	1501	B'ham	Cattle Point	Sec 12/Lot 4 [Brush weir]
04/01/39	Seaboard Investment	1501			Sec12/Lot 4 [Herring trap/brush weir]

Appendix B

Daily Catch, Center for Pacific Northwest Studies, PAF Box 99

Year	Trap #	Sockeye Catch
1917	547	63,094
1917	549	69,848
1917	557	45,303
1918	547	12,807
1918	549	14,603
1918	557	7,079
1919	547	5,162
1919	549	7,528
1919	557	8,642
1920	557	37,753
1921	547	16,782
1921	549	19,903
1921	557	21,858
1922	557	25,163
1923	547	3,519
1923	549	4,919
1923	557	5,343
1924	557	19,712
1925	547	13,985
1925	549	8,819
1925	557	15,496
1926	540	5,779
1926	557	13,627
1934	267	11,246
1934	264	8,692
1934	263	9,798
1934	261	5,555

Trap #557 belongs to Friday Harbor Packing Company or PAF for annual comparison.

Appendix C

Duwamish et al. Vs. United States